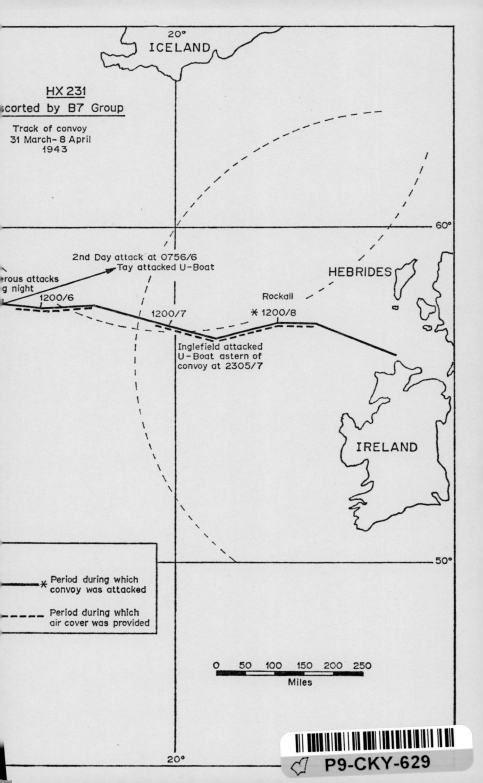

ICELAND

20°

## HX 231
### scorted by B7 Group

Track of convoy
31 March– 8 April
1943

2nd Day attack at 0756/6
Tay attacked U-Boat

HEBRIDES

erous attacks
g night

1200/6

Rockall

1200/7

✳ 1200/8

Inglefield attacked
U–Boat astern of
convoy at 2305/7

60°

IRELAND

50°

✳ Period during which
convoy was attacked

Period during which
air cover was provided

0   50  100  150  200  250
Miles

20°

# Crisis Convoy

By the same author


*Convoy Escort Commander*
*Maritime Strategy*
*Former Naval Person: Winston Churchill and the Royal Navy*

# Crisis Convoy

## The Story of HX231

**Vice-Admiral Sir Peter Gretton,**
K.C.B., D.S.O., O.B.E., D.S.C.

NAVAL INSTITUTE PRESS

Library of Congress Catalog Card No. 75–9027

ISBN 0–87021–925–1

Published and distributed in the United States
of America by the Naval Institute Press,
Annapolis, Maryland 21402

Printed in Great Britain

To my wife – ex W.R.N.S.

# Contents

# Contents

# Illustrations

(All these photographs, with the exception of 5(*b*) which was kindly provided by *Shell*, were supplied by courtesy of the Imperial War Museum.)

# Acknowledgements

*I should like to acknowledge with thanks the help received from many sources;* in particular, permission to reproduce quotations given by H.M. Stationery Office, the Public Records Office, the Imperial War Museum, the Naval Historical Branch, the Air Historical Branch, the Dutch Naval Historical Section and Professor J. Rohwer. Weidenfeld & Nicolson have also kindly allowed me to reproduce extracts from the *Admiral Dönitz Memoirs.*

# Introduction

There were several reasons why I determined to write this book. I hoped that it would be the first full story of an important Atlantic convoy to be written with the benefit of all the sources of information which have become available since the thirty-year rule relating to public records came into force in 1972.

Captain S. W. Roskill, in his official history of the 'war at sea' (see Bibliography), while making clear that the maintenance of the Atlantic life-line was the prerequisite to any continuation of the war, was unable, for reasons of space, to give more than a cursory account of Atlantic convoy passages. It is time that a full and authoritative story be written.

Not only will I use the reports of the escort commander and of the surface escorts, but also those of the Coastal Command aircraft which joined with such distinction in the defence of the convoy. There will be the report of the commodore of the convoy and of some of his ships, and especially of the ships which were lost and the stories of their survivors. In addition, the German records, which are very full, are now available; and so it has been possible to compare each side's account of particular incidents, to analyse the narratives and to sort out a number of hitherto unexplained events. Many, if not all, of the puzzling incidents have been resolved and it is now possible to look at the convoy passage as a whole, to determine its importance and to adjudicate on the outcome.

A second reason for writing this book was that I wanted to give a clear picture of the work of the merchant seamen during the Second World War which I do not think has yet been fully appreciated by the historians. These men did not belong to the armed forces and were rated as civilians. They were volunteers, though one must admit that if they decided to give up the sea, they were liable for conscription into the Forces. They endured great hardship, great discomfort and very great risk. I learnt only recently from a book, *Rescue Ships* (see Bibliography), that the merchant seaman had a higher casualty rate than any of the armed forces. Out of about 185,000 British merchant seamen, 32,952 lost their lives. This gives a casualty rate of 17 per cent, which can be compared with 9·3 per cent for the Royal Navy, 9 per cent for the Royal Air Force and 6 per cent for the Army. If the servicemen who manned the guns of the merchant ships are taken into account, the figures are even more startling. Men of the Defensive Equipped Merchant Service (or D.E.M.S. ratings, as they were colloquially called) were taken from the Royal Navy and the Royal Regiment of Maritime Artillery. They carried out some sterling work in ships which encountered enemy submarines and surface raiders in every part of the world. Their loss rate was high.

The third reason for this book was that I recently reread the *Memoirs* of Admiral Dönitz, who was head of the German U-boat arm throughout the war and who also took over command of the German Navy from Admiral Raeder in January 1943. From the first day of the war, indeed from earlier still, Dönitz was certain that Germany's only chance of defeating Britain was to cut the Atlantic life-line to America. He held firmly to this concept throughout the war, and I believe that he was right. Consequently, to Dönitz, Hitler's orders to station U-boats off Gibraltar, in the Mediterranean, off West Africa, in the Indian Ocean and even off Norway, where they aimed to stop supplies from reaching Russia, were unimportant side-lines which gravely jeopardized the main object. If he had had his way, every U-boat would have been in the North Atlantic.

So I chose a routine trade convoy in the North Atlantic, sailing from the United States and Canada to Britain at a time, in late March 1943, when the Battle of the Atlantic had reached a turning-point.

The story of convoy HX231 has all the ingredients of a typical oceanic confrontation. It was a large convoy: one of the first with over sixty ships. It had only a small surface escort and the operations around it took place before the defence had secured the advantage over the attack which came later. It was almost the first convoy to receive effective long-range air escort from the Liberators based in Iceland and Northern Ireland. A pack of twenty-one U-boats was directed on to the convoy, of which eighteen gained contact and seventeen started an attack. The convoy lost three ships which were torpedoed while in its columns and another three ships which had broken out or become involuntary stragglers were sunk separately, well clear of the convoy. The story of the survivors is indeed dramatic and heart-rending. There was no special rescue ship to pick up the men from the sunken ships and the escorts had to try to save them themselves. The weather was bad or very bad throughout the passage. Finally, the convoy was one of the first to have help later from one of the newly formed support groups; these roamed the Atlantic, ready to bring aid to convoys which were threatened or attacked.

I also chose convoy HX231, selfishly, because I was the escort commander and because I wanted to find out what really happened. I have been careful to write the narrative impersonally and, I trust, objectively; and I have been as ready to attribute blame as praise to my performance.

Finally, the six weeks which followed the arrival in harbour of convoy HX231, saw one of the most dramatic turns of fortune in the whole history of warfare. So I have tried to describe how the situation changed from one in which despair gripped Whitehall to one in which victory had been gained and the U-boats, if only temporarily, had been withdrawn from the North Atlantic

The chapter which follows will describe part of a typical attack on an ocean convoy by night and will introduce the reader to the human problems of life in a convoy escort and in the merchant ships under its protection.

# I

# The Blooding

---

It was about two hours after sunset on Sunday, 4 April. With a strong north-west wind on its port bow the convoy was pounding northwards through a rough sea; for the men in all the ships and escorts the tension was acute. The appalling March toll of Allied merchant vessels exacted by the German U-boat wolf-packs meant that the Battle of the Atlantic was now reaching what might well be a fatal climax.

There were sixty-one ships in the convoy, which was very large by the standards of the day, and all were heavily laden. Twenty-two were oil tankers, and the remaining freighters were loaded with a variety of cargoes ranging from bulk wheat and iron ore to tanks and aircraft. The sinister entry, 'explosives', appeared on the cargo manifest of several of the vessels, providing an additional terrifying hazard in the case of torpedo attack. The true value of the convoy and its cargo to a beleaguered Britain was beyond price.

Of the ships themselves there was rich variety: some were large and ponderous freighters which punched their way through the waves, creaking and groaning as they steamed on; and there were smaller ships, much livelier in movement, shuddering and shaking as they hit the troughs in the heavy sea. All were painted a uniform grey, no attempt having been made to copy the sophisticated camouflage schemes of the escort vessels.

The enemy had made contact with the convoy during the afternoon. At least three U-boats had been sighted on the horizon and the H/F D/F* office in the escort commander's ship had heard several others signalling briskly.

As soon as darkness had fallen, the escort commander had altered the convoy's course 45° to port to try to confuse the carefully positioned shadowing U-boats, the new course designed to

* High Frequency Direction Finding.

force some of them to choose to attack earlier than they intended (if they were to get in an attack at all), and some later. In three hours' time the original course would be automatically resumed.

Strain was additionally high among merchant ships' crews, for visibility had been good and the escorts had been seen dashing hither and thither; the distant dull rumble of depth-charge explosions could be heard. They could observe, too, what a weak escort had been provided; and no aircraft had appeared during the day to interfere with the U-boats' carefully deliberate assembly around them.

Warning had been given to the commodore of the convoy by the escort commander that they were likely to be in for a busy night, and before dark 'submarines in the vicinity' was hoisted in the commodore's ship. Throughout the passage the commodore was the essential link between the convoy and the escort commander and his task was an arduous one.

The formation in convoy HX231 was good and the station-keeping of the merchantmen was above average: usually the case when attack was threatened. 'Darken ship' (or the blackout) was excellent; there was not a sign of the chinks of light which so often gave away the position of ships to the enemy. The look-outs in every vessel, both of the escort and of the convoy, tensely scanned their allotted sector of the sea: in this weather it would not be easy to see the U-boats approaching on the surface, as the shadows of the waves could be confused with a conning-tower and the blown flecks of the wave-tops were not unlike a submarine's wake.

In the frigate *Tay*, the senior officer's ship, the escort commander, the captain of the ship and the staff stood on the open bridge, awaiting the attack which they knew must come soon. There had been much discussion about the probable run of events, and the placing of the escorts; finally, after a conference, the alteration of course to port had been decided.

There were yet further reasons for anxiety for although there was no moon, the aurora borealis had appeared on the northern horizon soon after sunset; the scene was as bright as day and the convoy felt particularly 'naked'. But more worrying still, it had been decided to strengthen the number of escort vessels on the convoy's port side, it being expected that the enemy would choose to attack down wind and sea; the starboard flank was consequently very weak, and with the unexpected silhouetting of the merchant ships against the northern lights it was now very possible that the attack might come in from the right.

In fact the corvette *Pink*, stationed on the starboard bow, was the only escort ship on that side. Ahead of the centre of the convoy was the corvette *Alisma*; the corvette *Loosestrife* was on the port bow; and on the port beam was the fourth corvette, *Snowflake*. *Tay* was on the port quarter where, it had been deduced at the conference, the attack would develop; and the only fast ship in the escort, the elderly destroyer *Vidette*, although rejoining at high speed after hunting a submarine astern, was still some four miles away.

The rough weather impaired the efficiency of the radar sets in detecting U-boats' attack approaches, so the escorts had been ordered to keep station closer than usual, about 5,000 yards, to their nearest merchant ships, and the conditions also held down the convoy's speed-made-good to 8 knots.

Such was the state of affairs before things began to happen: expectancy and a well-organized routine on board the escorts was the best means of meeting the unexpected.

In the *Tay* the ship's company was at defence stations, with only half the officers and men closed up, but every man off watch was lying fully dressed and ready to rush to his action station whenever the alarm bells rang. No less aware of the situation were the men in the boiler and engine rooms, well below the water-line, whose chances of survival if a torpedo struck were remote. There were indeed men who, unable to stand the thought of being trapped below when off duty, were trying to get some rest in corners of the wet, cold upper decks; and this fear was one of the worst problems facing a captain. Of those men who refused to sleep below many carried out their jobs efficiently, but others undoubtedly allowed their fears to affect the conduct of their duty. The captain would ask himself, 'Should A, B or C be put ashore as unsuitable?' To be reliable the answer needed the qualities of a psychologist as well as the professional judgment of a seaman.

One factor in such weather as this affected everyone, whether he were on or off watch, in the open or between decks: the sheer effort of keeping upright or secure. Walking, standing, sitting or even lying, whether in a corvette, frigate or destroyer, it was necessary to hold on fast to any convenient rail or stanchion, or to wedge one's body in a corner to keep it from crashing about.

For those on watch above decks, exposure to the weather was unending. On the bridge, at the guns, and on the quarter-deck aft, where the depth-charge crews waited for action, the men were faceless ghouls, wrapped in duffel coats, the hoods drawn over their heads and sometimes with sou'-westers added to give extra protection. As the spray came sweeping, rattling over them, each man ducked, then waited calmly until the arrival of the next wave's onslaught. If discomforts of this sort of existence did nothing to lessen the strain of waiting for the attack, the constant circulation of mugs of cocoa from the galley helped to warm bodies and so ease some of the tension.

This would be B7 Escort Group's first experience of U-boat attack since being re-formed at the turn of the year. There had been three months of hard training and rugged escort duty in appalling weather which had given confidence and sharp alertness. Yet, however great the preparation there was a nagging doubt in everyone, from the escort commander downwards, that now the testing time had come the training had been inadequate. In the case of at least one individual there was that unpleasant feeling in the pit of his stomach, sensed so keenly at such a crucial time as this. Nor was it difficult to guess the feelings of each captain, inevitably stationed on the bridge of each of the sixty-one wallowing merchant ships, wondering whether his ship would be the first to be hit.

The *Tay*, as the only ship fitted with H/F D/F, was able to detect if not interpret the signals streaming in from every direction from the gathering German U-boats. The officer in charge of the apparatus could give an approximate indication of where the enemy was assembling; and later that night as he gained experience he would prove to be able to judge when the next attack was

8

coming, as it became evident that many U-boats reported to 'Control' before beginning their attack run.

The voice pipe from bridge to H/F D/F was in constant use as bearings were passed and plotted on the chart in an effort to assess what the enemy was likely to do next: a battle of intelligence with the odds on the enemy. This one H/F D/F set for the whole of the escort group was under an intolerable strain and it could not possibly cover every frequency used by the enemy.

All the six ships in the group at least had their asdic* and radar sets in full working order. This was some consolation to the escort commander who had become all too accustomed during those three months after re-forming to some being out of action. With the asdic compartment sited on the bridge, it was tempting for the overworked officer of the watch and the captain to encourage the operator to ever greater efforts of concentration to the point of nagging. The radar operator on the other hand, shut up in his compartment under the aerial and well above the bridge, was for his own sake blessedly immune from any badgering.

The asdic's range this first night, like that of the radar, was much reduced by the high seas. The quick movement of the escort vessels and the bumping of the asdic dome at the bottom of the hull in the turbulent water had their effect in reducing the scope of the asdic beams; even the chances of the asdic's serving as a hydrophone with which to hear the U-boats on the surface were down to nil. And there was not the least hope of providing the radar 'fence' round the convoy, which in good weather with more escorts gave added protection. Indeed there were big gaps in the screen which the U-boats could penetrate probably undetected, hence the decision to keep the escorts closer to the convoy.

The prospects were certainly grim and the escort commander's chief hope had to lie in good drill and efficient teamwork as a means of reducing the number of ships to be sunk. He could not count upon being able to stop attacks.

A glimpse of the German situation at this stage – made possible by post-war scrutiny of enemy records – reveals a fascinating state

* Now called sonar.

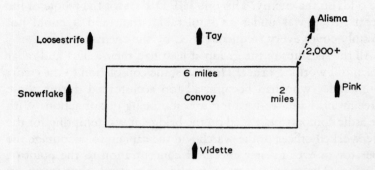

**DAY SCREENING STATIONS**

Loosestrife

Tay

Alisma

2,000+

6 miles

Convoy

2 miles

Snowflake

Pink

Vidette

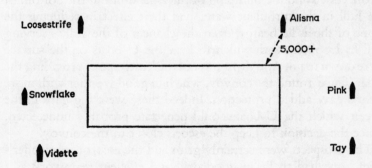

**NIGHT SCREENING STATIONS**

Loosestrife

Alisma

5,000+

Snowflake

Pink

Vidette

Tay

of affairs. Dönitz from Germany was urging the wolf-pack to make a great killing this first night, *before* the anticipated Allied aircraft had arrived to provide extra protection. This tactic, he wrongly surmised, would catch the escort on the hop. Of the twenty U-boats ordered to attack the convoy, eight were already in firm contact, awaiting their chance to approach and fire their torpedoes. Later in the night several more would gain contact.

Moreover, the weather conditions could hardly have been more favourable for the Germans on this first night of battle, and Dönitz was certainly right in urging as he did the utmost determination upon his U-boat captains.

About an hour after dusk an unknown ship in the convoy dropped a flare overboard. An escort raced in to try to put it out, but it was some time before the brightly burning light, which could be seen for miles, was quenched. The culprit was never discovered. Meanwhile it was not difficult to imagine the comments of the various ships, already exposed by the northern lights; understandable but specious rumours spread that a neutral ship in the convoy had been bent on helping the enemy; yet the escort commander's considerable fury over the affair was unnecessary, for the German records make no mention of the flare. Such incidents beset nearly every convoy passage. Sometimes, indeed, the results were serious; but usually they were of little consequence, and in this particular case, it was later realized, the U-boats were in such firm contact that the flare made little difference.

Then it was at 2208* that those on *Tay*'s bridge, from the ship's station on the port quarter of the convoy, saw a vivid white flash over the convoy's starboard side. Curiously, no explosion was heard and no signal was received. It was impossible to know what had happened. No rockets went up – two white rockets signalled that a ship had been torpedoed – and no star-shell or searchlights were seen that would indicate that an escort was counter-attacking.†

* 0008 G.M.T.
† Subsequent analysis showed that the flash was over five miles away.

Seven slow minutes passed, then the escort commander, unable to wait longer, grabbed the radio telephone and asked whether anything had happened. At once the *Pink* and the *Alisma* reported that two white rockets had just been fired, and the commodore of the convoy came in with the additional news that the leading ship of the twelfth column (No. 121, the *Shillong*) had just been torpedoed. From the bridge of his flagship, the *Tyndareus*, the commodore and his staff had been watching tensely for signs of an attack and listening for information on convoy wave radio. All escorts closed up at action stations. The battle was on.

The escort commander knew that the initial delay in reporting the torpedoing was very serious. It would have allowed the U-boat responsible to escape between the columns at high speed. The submarine had probably come in from ahead and penetrated the screen between the *Pink* and the *Alisma*, and had emerged from the convoy's starboard quarter which was unguarded.

At least eight minutes had passed after the torpedo-hit when the escort commander, after some hesitation, decided to order 'Half Raspberry', the code name of the operation normally carried out at night after an attack. This required all ships in the convoy to fire 'Snowflake' rockets to illuminate the whole area brilliantly. At the same time the escorts turned outwards and fired star-shells away from the convoy. The hope was that any submarine still within the perimeter of the convoy would be seen and any escaping outside it would be picked up by the escorts.

The escort commander had hesitated to give the order after seeing the white flash, because to illuminate the convoy unnecessarily in this way would be immensely dangerous; yet he had an uneasy feeling that something had happened. He should have trusted his instinct earlier.

The *Tay* was now also ordered to move over from the port to the starboard quarter of the convoy to try to cut off the U-boat's escape, but on her way to the new position she suddenly picked up a radar echo astern and valuable time was spent before it was identified by starshell search as the *Vidette* rejoining the formation.

By 2230, twenty-two minutes after the white flash had been

seen, it became very evident that 'Half Raspberry' had been ordered too late. As the northern lights were still bright, the rest of the escorts were then told to take up stations to cover equally the bow and the beam of the convoy, and the merchant ships were instructed to stop illuminations: a signal which for some time did not have full effect.

No sooner had the *Vidette*'s identity been established than *Tay* suddenly passed close to the rafts of the *Shillong*, surrounded by the bobbing red lights on the lifebelts of many men in the water. It was a ghastly and unforgettable experience: they were screaming for help, but it was only possible to shout back encouragement. In the middle of a battle there could be no question of stopping to pick up survivors, and no rescue ship was available. With promises that a vessel would come back later, the *Tay* rushed on; and indeed when 'Half Raspberry' was at last completed, the *Pink* was ordered to search astern for survivors until 0300, after which she had to return if nothing had been found. Her search was in fact without success and, as will be seen later, the fate of the men was a tragic one: their ship, loaded with zinc concentrate and wheat in bulk, had sunk with extraordinary speed.

There can be no clearer example of the appallingly difficult decisions that had to be made on such occasions as these. To have stopped the *Tay* to pick up survivors would have taken a long time and left a gap in the screen through which more U-boats might penetrate. It would also have forgone any chance of catching the enemy vessel responsible for the sinking. With more U-boats penetrating the gap, more ships and more men would be lost. The heart had to be hardened, and the bitter, logical rather than emotional, decisions taken; yet this did very little to relieve the later memories of the scene.

The escort group's first experience of a night attack had been an unhappy one. There seemed to have been an inexcusable delay in reporting a torpedoing after the white flash had been seen: a delay which seriously hindered the effectiveness of the search operations. The confusion over the identification of the *Vidette* had also been avoidable. Indeed the late decision to carry out

'Half Raspberry' had probably been an error of judgement which led merely to illuminating the convoy for the benefit of the next wave of attacking U-boats.

In the wisdom of later knowledge the delay in reporting had in fact not been as inexcusable as it appeared. The corvettes on the starboard side had certainly seen the flash, but for some inexplicable reason connected with the vagaries of sound waves in water, no explosion was heard. Furthermore, it was seven minutes before *Shillong* had been able to fire the two white alarm rockets, because the rocket-holder on her bridge had been crushed by blast. Nor was it possible at the time to determine from which side the torpedo had come; adjacent ships gave conflicting accounts, so the position of the culprit was even more difficult to estimate. (German reports reveal that in fact more than one torpedo was fired, so the convoy was lucky to have escaped with only one hit.)

The commodore wrote in his report: 'The northern lights were brilliant and the convoy should have been decimated by the U-boats'; and undoubtedly the rest of the ships shared his views. The strain on the officers and men of the merchant vessels was an increasing one and they still faced many hours of darkness. Other reports from the masters of the ships show that after the sinking of the *Shillong*, all kinds of imaginary incidents were logged. Two ships reported, wrongly, that other ships had been torpedoed; several U-boats 'sighted' proved to be shadows of waves or spume. Much more seriously, with tension at high pitch, three ships held councils of war, and made plans to leave the convoy as soon as possible. believing that they would be safer if sailing independently. Such plans, it will be seen, were tantamount to suicide.

On the enemy's side the tension was equally high. The day had been full of anxiety although, fortunately for them, no aircraft had appeared to interfere with the assembly of the wolf-pack.

The submarine *U630* had sighted the convoy in daylight, and had an accurate estimate of its position, course, and speed from several of the other boats. The visibility had been good but the sea rather rough, and in the conning-tower the captain, the officer of the watch and the four look-outs had been quickly soaked with sea water, some of which had gone down through the hatch into the hull. The U-boat had been at sea for some weeks and the ship's company was tired; despite this, morale was high and the captain had a reputation as a leader of men. In rough seas it was more comfortable to remain submerged, but a conscientious commanding officer knew that the best way of shadowing was to remain on the surface.

*U630* was in an excellent position to attack after dark, and helped by the northern lights, started an approach at about 2130.

To imagine the situation from the German captain's point of view is not by any means easy. He would not have realized how weak was the escort or the convoy's great size and importance. Probably he would be apt to exaggerate the capabilities of British radar, about which so many rumours had been flying around the U-boat fleet, and he would not appreciate that in this weather, radar detection range would not be more than 3,000–4,000 metres.

All in all it can be said that as in most operations in the U-boat war, the danger of approaching the convoy would seem greater to the attacking U-boat than the counter danger to the escort.

Once the approach run from a distance had begun, the men in the conning-tower would be straining to sight any of the convoy's ships. They would hope that after the attack they could remain on the surface and escape through the columns of the convoy, but those up top had to be ready, if a crash–dive became necessary, to rush down through the hatch.

The captain of *U630* made a short radio signal to Control, the shore-based U-boat headquarters, to warn them that he was about to attack. In this way it ensured that he would avoid collision with another boat coming in at about the same time. If two signals were received close together the second boat to signal would be ordered to delay the run-in for a short period.

After the attack, *U630*'s captain claimed in a signal to have sunk a freighter and a tanker; he must therefore have fired at least one more torpedo than the one which hit the *Shillong*. Further details of this U-boat's action are not known, for she herself was sunk before returning to harbour after the operations against the convoy, and the record entered in her war diary was therefore lost.

The British escort commander was satisfied neither with his own performance nor with that of his ships; he informed the ships accordingly in no uncertain terms. He expected an improvement when the next attacks came, and he got it.

# 2

# The Situation in March 1943

In early 1943, the war had reached a critical stage. In the Pacific, after many desperate night battles between American and Japanese naval forces, the island of Guadalcanal had been captured and the Americans were preparing for the taking of the Solomons and for an advance northwards. In New Guinea, the Japanese advance had also been checked. In the Indian Ocean area, Japan held all Burma, the road to China was cut, and the British and Indian armies were on the defensive, preparing for some future offensive.

On the Russian Front, the German thrust into the Caucasus had been thrown back and Stalingrad had been captured with the loss of the German Sixth Army; but the German advance was now stabilized on a defensible front and Russia desperately needed arms and supplies before embarking on an offensive. External supplies could come only by sea.

In North Africa, after the unexpectedly light casualties of operation 'Torch' – the invasion of Algiers, Oran, and Casablanca – the German resistance in Tunisia had stiffened and the Allied advance had been checked.

But public demands for a Second Front in Europe to take pressure off the Russians were still loud.

At Casablanca, in mid-January, President Roosevelt and Mr Churchill, assisted by their political and military advisers, worked hard to decide the next moves by the Allies. One controlling factor dominated every plan, however: the shortage of shipping.

Losses had been dreadful. No less than 7,790,000 tons of merchant shipping had been sunk in 1942, and the loss of seamen's lives had been grave. Merchant seamen rated as 'non-combatants', but their casualties were higher than many units of the armed forces. It is a great tribute to men of many countries, some neutral in the war, that they never flinched under the strain.

Shortage of ships was general. Ships were needed to take

supplies to Russia; ships in the Pacific for the war against Japan; and ships to carry supplies across the Atlantic to Britain, which was still the main base for all operations against the Germans and where a great American force of soldiers and airmen was steadily increasing in size preparatory to the assault on Europe: the list of shipping requirements was unending.

At the Casablanca Conference, Churchill had declared that 'the U-boat menace is still a very great one' and 'U-boat warfare takes first place in our thoughts'. He, at least, was under no illusions as to the danger and his statement that 'the defeat of the U-boat is the prelude to all effective aggressive operations' hit the nail on the head.

So an important result of Casablanca was an agreement to give first priority to the defeat of the U-boat, and among other decisions came one to make better use of the American aircraft already available in the Atlantic area. As a longer-term measure, too, it was decided to reduce merchant shipbuilding in Britain to 1,100,000 tons annually in order to increase the production of escort ships to defend the convoys. Shipbuilding in the United States and Canada would continue to increase and provided the only encouraging feature of a depressing situation.

The Admiralty monthly report for January 1943, shows that there had been over 100 U-boats at sea in the North Atlantic on any one day and that the aim was clearly to cut communications across the ocean. The report ends ominously: 'The critical phase of the U-boat war in the Atlantic cannot be long postponed. A bolder and more reckless strategy and concentration against shipping of immediate military importance are the keynotes of enemy present policy.'

The same authority reported at the end of February that the concentration of U-boats in the North Atlantic continued and that one convoy had been attacked heavily outside range of air cover (i.e. in the 'air gap'). It ended: 'The months ahead are most critical and success is by no means assured.'

Another of the fruits of Casablanca was a grand 'Atlantic Convoy Conference' which was held in Washington D.C. during the first twelve days of March. Opened by the formidable

American Chief of Naval Operations, Admiral King, it was attended by senior officers of the American, British, and Canadian navies, of the Royal Air Force and the Royal Canadian Air Force, of the U.S. Army, whose aircraft still flew on A/S* operations in many areas, and by representatives of the Shipping Administrations. The results of the conference were most satisfactory, and there was general agreement on the measures needed.

Among other decisions was one to form a new North-Western Atlantic Command under a Canadian officer. Another was to keep the same escort ships in the same groups so that the groups were more likely to remain intact and thus be able to reach higher standards of training. Most important of all was a unanimous agreement to press strongly for more American very long-range aircraft to be sent to the Atlantic, and particularly to the north-western area, where there was not one V.L.R. aircraft operating. None of these improvements, however, would take effect for weeks if not months, and meanwhile the Allies were facing further disasters.

In the first three weeks of March, the situation at sea deteriorated sharply. Winter storms damaged escorts and prevented aircraft from flying to the convoys. Several major prolonged attacks on convoys were made and in the first ten days of the month forty-one ships were sunk and in the second, forty-four: a total of over 500,000 tons which was half the *annual* British shipbuilding effort.

At the end of March, the Admiralty report commented: 'The significance of the period up to the twentieth of March was that it appeared possible that we should not be able to continue convoy as an effective defence against the enemy pack attacks.'

Roskill (the official historian of the 'war at sea') writes:

> 'No one can look back on that month without feeling something approaching horror at the losses suffered ... what made the losses even more serious than the bare figures indicate, was that nearly two thirds of the ships sunk during the month were sunk in convoy. ... Where would the Admiralty turn if the convoy system lost its effectiveness?

* Anti-submarine.

They did not know, but they must have felt, though none admitted it, that defeat stared them in the face.'

The situation appeared grim indeed, especially as on 3 March, the Paymaster General (Professor Lindemann, later Lord Cherwell) had warned that 'we are consuming $\frac{3}{4}$ million tons more than we are importing. In *two months*, we could not meet our requirements if this continued.'

This was the situation, then, when on 25 March the main portion of convoy HX231 sailed from New York, heavily laden with supplies of every kind for the United Kingdom. Times were critical and perhaps it was just as well that the crews of the ships and the companies of the escort vessels did not realize how very critical they were!

On 9 March, Rear-Admiral Edelsten, who was in charge of the anti-U-boat and Trade Divisions of the Admiralty Staff and who ran day-to-day operations in Whitehall, had written a strong note to the First Sea Lord, Admiral Sir Dudley Pound. His first paragraph read:

> 'The foreseen has come to pass. The Director of Naval Intelligence reported on 8 March that the Tracking Room will be "blinded" in regard to U-boat movements for some considerable period, perhaps extending to months.'

It is very difficult to get information about the extent to which the British were able to crack German codes and ciphers, for the papers have not been released. But Edelsten's report clearly indicates that a successful period when, presumably, the British had managed to break the German codes, had ended and it would therefore no longer be possible to route convoys clear of the U-boats whose positions had been obtained from the cryptographers. Reliance would henceforth have to be placed on taking bearings of radio signals made by the U-boats, which in any case was only an approximate method, the value of which had been lowered recently by a reduction of as much as 75 per cent in the volume of U-boat transmissions from sea. A grave situation had been made worse by a defeat in the battle between the cryptographers, for we know from the Dönitz *Memoirs* that the Germans were able at this time to read many of the British codes and ciphers and to know the position, course, and speed of all convoys. Moreover they were reading the Admiralty U-boat situation reports and were thus enabled to know where the British thought that their U-boats were!

We now know that there were 116 U-boats at sea in March and 111 in April, but the Admiralty Tracking Room then had only a very vague idea of their position and exact numbers.

Admiral Edelsten, in the report already mentioned, went on to suggest four different courses of action to counter the crisis. These were, first, to accelerate the provision of V.L.R. aircraft to Coastal Command; second, to accelerate the provision of escort carriers with the convoys; third, to intensify the bombing of U-boat bases in the Bay of Biscay; and fourth, to obtain operational use of the Azores for anti-submarine aircraft. It will be noted that three of these suggestions would have provided better air escort for convoys.

But all were comparatively long-term palliatives and would not immediately affect the issue in the Atlantic.

In addition, the Commander-in-Chief Bomber Command, Sir Arthur Harris, was strongly averse to releasing even one Liberator aircraft to Coastal Command. He had a particular objection to losing any aircraft fitted with the new centimetric radar (A.S.V. III) which had an improved ability to detect surfaced U-boats at night and in bad weather, and he fought hard to acquire every single V.L.R. aircraft for his Command.

These quotations from a paper which he sent to the Prime Minister's anti-U-Boat Committee on 29 March 1943, show the extent of his obsession.

'In view of the very large number of U-boats which the enemy will operate in the coming months, the proportion of his successes which would be eliminated by accepting the Admiralty proposals [to release more Liberators to Coastal Command and to bomb the U-boat bases in the Bay of Biscay] seems to be so small as to be negligible. The effect of them on the Bomber Offensive would certainly be catastrophic. . .

'In the present case it is inevitable that at no distant date the Admiralty will recognize that U-boats can effectively be dealt with only by attacking the sources of their manufacture... It cannot be pointed out too strongly that in the Bomber Offensive lies the only hope of giving really substantial help to Russia this year or in the foreseeable future; that its effect can be substantiated by incontrovertible evidence; and that if it is reduced to lesser proportions by further diversion of large numbers of bomber aircraft for seagoing defensive duties, it will fail in its object and the failure may well extend to the whole of the Russian campaign. This in my opinion would be a far greater disaster than the sinking of a few extra merchant ships each week...

'I feel, however, that too much emphasis is being given to the possibility of locating U-boats by means of A.S.V. (radar) and too little to the difficulty of attacking them successfully when they are located. Our experience, which is considerable, is that even expert crews find it no easy matter to attack with accuracy even a city by means of H2S. I am therefore rather sceptical of the prospects of inexperienced crews with A.S.V. Indeed, I feel that the provision of aircraft equipped with this apparatus will mark the beginning rather than the end of the difficulties involved in sinking U-boats...'

There was no doubt that the Naval Staff were wrong to press for more bombing of U-boat bases in the Bay of Biscay. Bitter experience was quickly to show that once the concrete U-boat shelters had been completed, the U-boats were invulnerable. Not one submarine was even delayed by these attacks which, in addition, devastated the French towns nearby.

But everything else which Harris said in these paragraphs proved to be wrong and usually exactly the opposite was the case. It was fortunate that he did not have his own way. The official historian of the 'war at sea' has written:

'This writer's view is that in the early spring of 1943, we had a very narrow escape from defeat in the Atlantic; and that, had we suffered that defeat, history would have judged that the main cause had been the lack of two more squadrons of very long range aircraft for convoy escort duties.'

This reveals the Harris philosophy in its true colours, for had the Battle of the Atlantic been lost, there would have been no import of metals to build bombers and no aviation spirit to enable the bombers to fly.


At the headquarters of the U-boat command, the Allied situation did not look so desperate to Admiral Dönitz. German intelligence had badly overestimated the probable production of merchant ships in North America and reckoned that from early 1943, the building of new ships would exceed the maximum losses which the Germans expected to inflict on Allied shipping. But in fact, the total amount of Allied shipping available continued to drop until July 1943 and, what is more, the demands on shipping continued to rise. More ships were needed in the Atlantic for the Russian convoys and to build up supplies in Britain for the coming invasion of Europe. In the Pacific, the demand seemed to be endless and it increased as the Americans advanced.

Also Dönitz was very worried by the unexplained losses of U-boats, mainly to air attack which had started to mount in the autumn of 1942. The radar search receivers were suspect.

The principle of radar, as is well known, is that an electro-magnetic wave is transmitted which hits the target and bounces back. The receiver is able to measure the interval and hence obtain the range, and a bearing can also be obtained of the target.

If the wavelength of the transmission is known, however, a search receiver can be fitted in the target which will give warning when an enemy is transmitting in its direction. A U-boat could then dive. By 1942, all U-boats were fitted with a search receiver which gave warning of the approach of aircraft or escorts which were transmitting on the metric wave. But the British had developed a new radar set working on a wavelength of 10 cm., which had many advantages. It gave a better picture of the target and was able to detect U-boats at greater range. The German scientists, however, had never believed in the technical possibility of building such a set, and as a result no search receiver had been developed which would give warning of their enemy's approach.*

U-boats were liable to be caught by surprise, particularly by aircraft fitted with the new set, and losses had been severe. Only in March 1943, did Dönitz receive practical proof of the new situation when the *U333*, in transit across the Bay of Biscay, was illuminated by an aircraft fitted with the new radar, against which no warning had been obtained.

Despite these anxieties, Dönitz was encouraged by the heavy sinkings of March 1943; he knew that he could continue to keep over 100 U-boats at sea during April, and he had confidence in his commanding officers who were well trained. Most of them, however, were from the second generation of submarine commanders, for the aces who had started the war were now either lost or resting in posts ashore.

Moreover, he was fortified by the knowledge that the 'Milch Cow' U-boats – large craft which acted as tankers for refuelling other submarines – had been most successful in prolonging the length of operational cruises. One of the 'Milch Cows', for example, had refuelled no less than twenty-seven U-boats in the first five days of March, in an area in mid-Atlantic which was free from the danger of air patrols and which had proved safe from attack.

Before returning to convoy HX231, however, we should discuss the system of Allied convoys and the methods by which their protection was provided against German submarine pack attacks.

The convoys across the North Atlantic were divided into two classes, fast and slow, though the so-called fast convoys were somewhat flatteringly named, as they could seldom manage an average of nine knots! The eastbound loaded convoys were called HX

---

* An R.A.F. Pathfinder bomber which was fitted with centimetric radar was shot down on 2 February 1943. Examination revealed the new set, and at once, the German Navy started to work on a new search receiver. But it was never successful and took many months to develop.

(Halifax) if fast, and SC (Sydney, Cape Breton) if slow; the west-bound convoys in ballast were called ON if fast and ONS if slow.

The convoy cycle (or frequency of sailing) was a complicated matter to determine. It depended on the number of ships of various speeds which were estimated to be ready to sail, on the size of the convoy, and on the number of escort groups which were available to protect them.

At the time of the passage of HX231, HX and ON convoys sailed every six days and SC and ONS convoys every eight. Much controversy had raged about the number of ships in these convoys, for as the size increased, the number of convoys needed to transport a given total of ships across the ocean decreased and with it the number of escort groups required. Early in 1943, Professor Blackett, the brilliant Head of Naval Operational Research, had shown that owing to the shape of these convoys – they were wide but had no great depth – the number of ships included could be increased considerably, with only a small increase in the perimeter and hence in the number of escorts required. This self-evident truth had not been well received by the Naval Staff which argued that an increase in size led to difficulties in station-keeping and in manoeuvring and control, and any change was resisted. But these disadvantages were imaginary and by the spring of 1943, the Naval Staff agreed reluctantly to increase the fast convoys to sixty ships while keeping the SC and ONS convoys to forty. Results were to show that Blackett was right and, later on, convoys with as many as 150 ships sailed safely across the sea.

HX231, as one of the first sixty-ship convoys, was six sea miles across and two sea miles in depth. (There were thirteen columns, each containing four or five ships; the columns were 1,000 yards apart and ships in column were 400 yards apart.)

German policy had been evolved by Dönitz between the wars, when he had written a book describing his plans in some detail. But no one who mattered can have read the book and nothing was done. His plans had been improved and refined by three years' wartime experience. Knowing from the cryptographers the position of each convoy and its course and speed, it was not difficult for the U-boat command to station a reconnaissance group of U-boats, spaced so that no convoy could pass through the line without being sighted or heard on the submarines' hydrophones. Most of the groups, containing about ten U-boats, were stationed in mid-Atlantic so that they could attack convoys sailing in either direction. There they were able to take advantage of the 'air gap' where only the few V.L.R. aircraft could reach. Once a convoy was sighted its position was signalled to Control at the U-boat headquarters, which immediately informed the remaining U-boats of the pack and also probably ordered another pack to approach the position. The first sighting U-boat remained in touch as 'contact keeper' and was not allowed to attack until ordered to do so by Control. Each U-boat reported when it gained touch with the convoy and when sufficient boats were in contact, Control ordered them to attack. The night, when aircraft did not operate, was the favourite time. U-boats came in on the surface and with their small silhouette were very difficult to see. They approached from ahead, from the bows and from either beam, and their speed and manœuvrability allowed them to enter the columns of the convoy and fire torpedoes without fear of collision with the merchant ships.

There were disadvantages to the system, some of which fortunately were not understood in Germany. First, all the radio signalling alerted the surface escort ships which, when fitted with H/F D/F sets, could get bearings of the transmitting submarines. The Admiralty, through a chain of shore-based H/F D/F stations scattered around the Atlantic, was also warned that something was afoot.

It was here that the Admiralty Tracking Room, manned by Rodger Winn (then Q.C., later Lord of Appeal), and Commander (now Vice-Admiral) Norman Denning, became so important. All the data available were analysed and the results sent by telephone to the Commander-in-Chief Western Approaches at Liverpool, and to the Commander-in-Chief Coastal Command at Northwood in Middlesex. Information from the shore H/F D/F stations, information from cryptographers, reports from ships and from aircraft, and intelligence from other channels were all collated. The work of the Tracking Room was, because of its secrecy, known to few, but its influence on the war at sea, and on the Battle of the Atlantic especially, was very great.

A second disadvantage of the pack attack was that the U-boats had to travel on the surface by day in order to get into position for the night, because their submerged speed was too low to allow this when dived. When surfaced, they could be sighted by aircraft around the convoy and forced to submerge or be attacked. Hence the great importance of escort aircraft and of filling the 'gap'.

Third, the improved centimetric radars, fitted by March 1943 in all ocean escorts, were capable of detecting submarines on the surface at a range, with a calm sea, of about four miles. A well-trained and skilfully handled escort group could, therefore, in good weather at night form a radar 'fence' around the convoy, and hope, if no gaps were left by one means or another, to detect the submarines as they attacked and to force them to break off the approach and dive.

The defensive perimeter of a convoy of the size of HX231 was about sixty miles, so that theoretically, in perfect weather, six escorts could nearly form a firm radar screen. But, of course, if attacks were made simultaneously, gaps would occur in the screen through which more submarines could slip undetected.

By day U-boats could attack only when submerged, so that after night action they would have to steam at best speed on the surface to gain bearing in order to get back into position to approach from ahead. Here again, an aircraft circling the convoy outside the visibility range of the surface escorts, was invaluable for 'keeping the U-boats' heads down'.

The range of the asdic was considerably less than that of the radar; and it was also far less consistent. Fish, water rips, and wakes were all inclined to give echoes, which sounded like a submarine, and in some water conditions the range of the asdic was much reduced from the usual maximum of about 2,000 yards.

With this detection range it was quite impossible for a normal-sized escort group to form any asdic fence around the convoy. Instead, ships would be stationed on the bows, ahead and on the

beams and by zigzagging unpredictably, hope at least to make a
U-boat's approach difficult.

So submerged attack by day, by a submarine which had succeeded in getting ahead of the convoy, was a comparatively simple
operation; and after a successful attack the search for the offender
was badly hampered by the hulls and wakes of the ships in convoy
near which the U-boat would hide submerged before making
good its escape.

Dönitz liked to concentrate two groups on the convoys he was
attacking, as he found by experience that twenty was about the
maximum number of U-boats which could be easily controlled
around a convoy without confusion or risk of collision, which
was not unknown.

One other development on our side, brought in force regularly
at the end of March 1943, was the use of the surface support force
for increasing the strength of the escort of threatened convoys.
The move had long been planned, but ships had not been available
without denuding the close escort groups unacceptably. Now, the
convoys to Russia had been temporarily suspended and the ships
so released were formed into support groups for the Atlantic.

By listening to German radio traffic it was possible to guess
which convoys were threatened with attack and then to divert a
support group to their aid. If no warning were received, it was
hoped that a group would be in position to speed to the help of a
convoy under attack. In the case of HX231, we shall see that the
Fourth Support Group had been ordered to sail from Iceland to
join the convoy before the first sighting reports had been received;
but the appalling weather prevented its arrival before the close
escort had fought on alone for two days and two nights.

There were several other matters which, by the start of April,
had been improved on the Allied side. A modest increase had been
obtained in the efficiency of the surface escort groups, for previously training had been very difficult, due to short 'lay-over'
periods in harbour between convoys and to constant changes in
the composition of groups. Standards had been very low for these
reasons and the improvement, which was probably one of the
biggest single factors in the eventual victory, was due greatly to

the drive of the tough and astute Commander-in-Chief, Admiral Sir Max Horton, who took over in November 1942.

There were improvements in the air side too. By early April there were nine V.L.R. Liberators based in Iceland and nine at Aldergrove in Northern Ireland. These few planes were to do much to close the 'air gap' and to provide close air escort for convoys all over the North Atlantic. The efficiency of all Coastal Command aircraft was starting to improve steadily, due to the arrival of Air Chief Marshal Sir John Slessor as Commander-in-Chief in February 1943. His predecessor had had an extraordinary aversion to 'standard' methods of attacking U-boats and did not seem to agree with exercises: he considered each attack an individualistic matter which must not become stereotyped. Slessor soon reversed this nonsensical policy and although he was not able to institute regular training in attacking U-boats until the end of April 1943, he had earlier made it clear that he was not prepared to tolerate the 'hang up' of depth-charges and the dropping of depth-charges set to safe which had occurred far too often during attacks on German submarines. The procedure by which aircraft were homed on to convoys by the use of H/F D/F was also becoming more efficient and more widely used, and as a result the number of aircraft which failed to find their convoys and had to report 'not met' began to decrease.

Lastly, Slessor had finally resolved the argument over the employment of the V.L.R. and L.R. aircraft. For some time, the supporters of the so-called offensive school, led by Slessor's predecessor, who advocated using these aircraft on great sweeps of the ocean searching for submarines, had possessed much too much influence. The idea was attractive as it gave the impression of offensive action, but its practical possibilities of success were few and it was a waste of time and effort.

Where the aircraft were needed was around any convoy which was either threatened or actually under attack. In this way the U-boats would be prevented from either sighting the convoy or, where they were already in contact, from gaining a suitable position from which to fire. There were not enough aircraft to escort every convoy all the time, and even if the numbers were available it would have been a waste of valuable aircraft. Much depended therefore on good intelligence, so that air escort could be provided as soon as there was any indication that a convoy was in potential danger of being sighted by U-boats.

On 19 February Slessor had quickly decided the issue by his instructions that the close escort of threatened or attacked convoys was to receive first priority, though he added that when the available number of aircraft allowed, he hoped to resume the offensive.

When convoy HX231 sailed from New York on 25 March 1943, although the situation was grave, there were chinks of light ahead which promised improved protection.

# 3

# From New York
# to the Meeting with the Ocean Escort

Forty-nine ships, which formed part of convoy HX231 sailed from New York on Thursday, 25 March 1943, at 0850 (local time: +5).* One of the ships was bound for Halifax (Nova Scotia) and another for St John's (Newfoundland); all the rest were bound for the United Kingdom. The commodore of the convoy was Admiral Sir Charles Ramsey, who had until his recent retirement been the Commander-in-Chief, Rosyth. He flew his flag in the fine Blue Funnel ship *Tyndareus*. The vice-commodore was Captain McColm of the *Jamaica Planter*, which joined later with the Halifax portion; and the rear-commodore was the captain of the tanker of the *Laurelwood*, leading ship of the fourth column. The nominal speed of the convoy was 9 knots and, in fact, it achieved 8·74 knots over the whole length of its seventeen-day voyage.

For the passage from New York until the Halifax portion joined off the Nova Scotian coast, about 150 miles east of Sable Island, there were three Canadian escorts, two corvettes, the *Saskatoon* (K158) acting as senior officer and *Quesnel* (K133), as well as one Bangor-class minesweeper, the *Kenora* (J281).

It was a weak escort and its ships were slow, but fortunately the U-boats had left the Western Atlantic seaboard and the risk of attack was very small. In 1942, just after America had entered the war, the U-boats had enjoyed their second 'happy times' when they caught the United States unprepared and had inflicted enormous losses on shipping. But when convoys had been started and when a few escorts and some air cover had been provided, the losses had quickly reduced and by the start of 1943, the U-boats were again assembling in mid-Atlantic.

* All times will be given in local time, i.e. the time of the zone which the convoy had reached.

Anyhow the passage along the American coast was uneventful except for some very bad weather and the departure of the stand-by escort tanker, the *F. J. Wolfe*, which had to return to harbour with engine trouble. This left only the *British Ardour* as the tanker fitted with hoses and pumps for refuelling escorts at sea, and it might have had serious consequences. Three other ships, the *Georgian*, the *Noah Webster*, and the *Saluta*, also left the convoy but without informing the commodore, who noted in his report that they had left for reasons unknown. In fact, each one had mechanical trouble of some sort or other and each regained harbour safely. It was not a very satisfactory start for Commodore Ramsey, however, to lose three of his ships in this way. At 1400 (+4) on 29 March, four days after the convoy had left New York, another escort group brought the Halifax portion of thirteen ships, under the command of the vice-commodore, to join the main body. These ships had already been allotted pendant numbers which indicated their position in the convoy; and they should have quickly taken up their new stations.

The extreme cold had frozen the signal halliards of the ships, however, and ice had broken the commodore's signalling mast. Flag signals were impossible and all messages had to be passed by light. Visibility was poor, so that the process of forming up the convoy was very slow and ships were not in station before dark. However, collisions were avoided, and the next day, the new escort from Halifax, which consisted of the ex-American destroyer *Buxton* (H96), the senior officer, the corvette *Chictoutimi* (K156) and the *Quesnel* which had stayed on with the convoy after the other two ships of the New York escort had been detached, succeeded in getting them into some sort of shape. There were thus still three Canadian escorts, the group being slightly strengthened by the inclusion of the *Buxton*, which was one of the fifty 'lend lease' destroyers which had been exchanged for base rights in the British West Indies.

Meanwhile, four ships from Newfoundland had left St John's on the afternoon of the same day, 29 March, under the escort of the corvette *Pink*.

A very independent-minded Norwegian ship, the *Scebeli* had

also been ordered to join the section of the convoy sailing from St John's, but she appears to have disregarded her instructions and set off eastwards on her own. She radioed later a request either to be given a rendezvous with the convoy or a stragglers' route to follow. She was offered the choice of either, but did not keep the rendezvous and sailed to the United Kingdom on the stragglers' route. It is sad to read that this same ship was torpedoed and sunk only a few weeks later when straggling from a westbound convoy. Retribution quickly caught up with the persistent stragglers.

A few hours after the *Pink* had left St John's with her section, the remainder of the ocean escort, consisting of five ships of B7 Group* sailed for the rendezvous with the convoy at 'Westomp' (Western Ocean meeting place). The last links of the complicated process of assembling and escorting an eastbound convoy were now falling into place. It always seemed to be a miracle of organization that this pattern was produced with such regularity and with so few mistakes.

There were two naval bases in Newfoundland, one at St John's and one at Argentia. The Royal Canadian Navy ran the St John's base and had worked hard to provide the repair and training facilities needed. An elderly British repair ship, the *Greenwich*, had been stationed at St John's for some time and did much good work, but the facilities were gradually being transferred ashore. By the spring of 1943, an efficient and well-provided base with a small dry dock which would take a corvette had been set up and could undertake all normal repairs. St John's also had the advantage of being close to the 'bright lights' where officers and men could get some relaxation after the arduous ocean passages. The local people were most hospitable and St John's managed well with the flood of extra visitors. But the weather, especially in winter, was very bad and hindered the repair organization.

At Argentia, the United States Navy had set up a modern base
* British escort groups were suffixed 'B', Canadian groups 'C' and the American groups, which were gradually being phased out of the North Atlantic, 'A'.

with an airfield, a floating dock large enough to take a destroyer, and a modern repair ship well fitted with the latest equipment. The service was good, but the base was not very popular, as there was not even a local village to recall civilization and the surrounding country was bare and bleak.

After this digression, we return to B7 Group *en route* from St John's to Westomp. Some exercises were carried out but the cold weather and rough seas reduced their value and made them very unwelcome to officers and men. Opportunity was also taken to practise communication both by R/T and by light with Canso* aircraft from the bases of the Royal Canadian Air Force in New-foundland.

Co-operation between ships and aircraft in the North-West Atlantic was still at the same low level as it had been in the Eastern Atlantic over a year back and results were disappointing. The ships of B7 Group had made great efforts to bridge the gap between the airmen and the sailors and the atmosphere was improving; the communication exercise was valuable and some progress was achieved.

The reported position of the convoy was over sixty miles in error and this and the thick fog, which was a regular feature of the Grand Banks at that time of year, delayed the meeting very considerably. An H/F D/F bearing of the *Buxton* had to be taken before the convoy was found after dark on 30 March. The turn-over from the senior officer in the *Buxton* took some time and the information received was not entirely satisfactory; the convoy was still in some confusion and there was even doubt as to how many ships were present.

However, the exchange was eventually concluded and at 2135, the three Canadian escorts left for St John's, taking with them the *Lady Rodney* which was bound for that port.

Next day, 31 March, was spent by B7 Group in shepherding the ships into their correct stations, in counting heads, and in exchanging information with Commodore Ramsey. In the after-noon, the *Pink* with the four ships from St John's turned up, and

* Canso: a Canadian-built Catalina flying-boat.

34

by dusk, the whole convoy had been mustered, sorted out and found to contain sixty-one ships.

The size of these convoys, as has been mentioned already, was very great – six sea miles across and two miles deep – and even in moderate visibility it was often impossible for all ships to be able to see each other. Flag signalling became a slow process, especially at the start of the passage before much practice had been obtained. It was not possible to use radio, as the medium wave available would give away the convoy's position.

Of the sixty-one ships, there were thirty-six British, fourteen American, six Norwegian, three Dutch, one Swedish and one Panamanian. Included in these were no less than twenty-two tankers, with loads of heavy fuel oil for the Royal Navy, of diesel oil, of motor spirit, of aviation spirit, of alcohol, of vaporizing oil and of one cargo which was described as 'burning oil'.

The thirty-nine dry cargo ships carried a wide variety of loads. There was wheat and sugar, both in bags and bulk, and one ship had 10,000 tons of dates from Basra. There was zinc, iron ore, copper, and chemicals of various kinds in bulk and there were ships loaded with timber. There were cargoes of explosives; there were trucks, tanks, and aircraft; and landing craft were stowed on some upper decks. And there was also a mass of general cargo with every conceivable variety of stores ranging from citrus fruit to condensed milk, from beef powder to machinery. A total of just over 600,000 tons sailed of which 523,000 tons arrived safely at their destinations.

Over and above these ships and their cargoes, there were two U.S. naval supply ships carrying specialized stores for the United Kingdom. Some ships carried passengers, one or two having a many as 100 aboard; while there were bags of mail distributed among some of the ships.

The convoy would bring a very important addition to the scanty reserves of food and raw materials in Britain and would ease the task of the hard-pressed officials in the Ministries of Food and Supply. Wheat was especially important, as bread was the only unrationed food and it was essential to maintain good reserves.

It was the largest convoy which B7 Group had yet met, and the escorts were suitably impressed by the magnitude and importance of their task.

The group had re-formed in January 1943 after a succession of mishaps and tragedies which had culminated in the loss of the group leader and his ship. The new leader had had only one passage in charge of a convoy and its escort, but he was widely experienced in North Atlantic convoy work. He had worked from Londonderry in command of an old 'S' class destroyer for over twelve months from January 1941, and then from Liverpool in an old 'W' class destroyer for most of the rest of 1942. Before 1941, he had been first lieutenant of two destroyers, one on east coast convoy work from the Firth of Forth to the Thames, and the other working from Scapa where the Home Fleet sometimes carried out escort work

These long years had instilled a deep instinct which could recognize and understand the difficulties of merchant ships in convoy and the problems of handling large convoys in all weathers. It had given, too, the skill needed to use the escorts and the aircraft to the best advantage.

While lectures on convoy problems and exercises on tactical tables all helped, it was only the years of hard slogging across the Western Ocean which gave the ingrained skills needed. They were highly specialized qualities which required a mind which was quick to react to circumstances, ready to absorb new ideas, able to use the imagination which put itself in the enemy's place, and above all eager to draw on the distilled experience of many ocean passages. While personal qualities were obviously important, the experience was essential.

Between the beginning of January and the end of March, the group had run regularly between Derry and Newfoundland. The weather had been uniformly atrocious, and partly due to this not one of the five convoys which it had escorted had been attacked. There was little to show for three months' running except much rust and some weather damage, but there was the comforting feeling of convoys safely delivered to their destinations.

In January, when the group re-formed, standards of training had been low, and much hard work had been put in to improve them. Before sailing on each convoy passage, harbour training was carried out in Derry. The depth-charge crews and the guns crews were exercised in realistic shore trainers and the asdic team was given excellent practice in a double-decker bus fitted with a synthetic trainer. This benefited not only the asdic operators, but the plotting-table crew, the control officer and the commanding officer himself.

Before leaving on each escort duty, two or three days and nights were spent exercising off the entrance to the River Foyle, working with submarines, firing at targets and carrying out the multitude of jobs which might fall to a convoy escort. In fact, the men sometimes complained that they felt more tired after the pre-convoy exercises than after the convoy passage itself!

These three months had helped to weld the ships into a closely knit group. The escort commander's own ship, the destroyer *Duncan*, was refitting; so he was temporarily embarked in the frigate *Tay* with a small staff of one navigating lieutenant who acted as operation officer, and one sub-lieutenant as H/F D/F officer. Both were Royal Naval Volunteer Reserve officers. Both were very competent and loyal, and the results were excellent. One is now a rural dean, having joined the Church after the war, and the other an eminent geologist at Oxford. As a result of this influx, the *Tay*'s cabins and wardroom space became rather crowded, but by the exercise of considerable tolerance both sides got on well together.

The situation was in fact something of an advantage for the escort commander for, without his own ship to command, he could spend more time in the other ships of the group during exercise periods; and so by his personal influence he could put across his points of view and his requirements at this formative time in the group's history.

The captain of the *Tay* (K232), Lieutenant-Commander R. E. Sherwood, R.N.R. was an experienced convoy man, having commanded a corvette before getting the *Tay*. He was a proficient seaman with a long career in the Irish cross-channel services. At

37

sea on convoy duty, it was a great advantage to have the benefit of his advice.

These 'River' class frigates were an improvement on the corvettes, though designed on the same lines. They were faster, with a speed of 20 knots; they had two 4-in. guns; they were larger, with a tonnage of 1,370 compared with the corvettes' 980, and their complement was 140 men instead of 100.

The old destroyer *Vidette* (D48) was commanded by Lieutenant R. Hart of the regular Navy, who had spent most of the war in destroyers in the Mediterranean. But he had learnt quickly in the three months' running in the Atlantic and he was both keen and capable. One of the *Vidette*'s boilers had been removed and extra fuel tanks substituted, so she was now known as a long-range escort destroyer. Her maximum speed was 26 knots, which was ample for the average weather in the North Atlantic. The *Vidette* was a happy ship with a fine spirit.

There were four corvettes in the group. The *Alisma* (K185) was commanded by an Australian, Lieutenant-Commander M. G. Rose, R.A.N.V.R. and the remaining officers also came from 'down under', though the ship's company was from the United Kingdom. This unusual combination worked very well. The Australians had had the advantage of a longer and more thorough training in anti-submarine warfare than had their British opposite numbers and the A/S standards of the *Alisma* were high. Rose, an accountant in private life, had been in command for some time and had escorted many convoys.

The *Pink* (K137) was commanded by another experienced escort man, Lieutenant Robert Atkinson, R.N.R., who had served at sea in the merchant service before 'swallowing the anchor' and taking up a business career ashore. Very determined and competent, his views on life were sometimes a little too serious for his colleagues, but a cordial relationship was soon established and the *Pink* fitted well into the group as a very capable ship.

The captain of the *Snowflake* (K211) was another Australian, Lieutenant Harold Chesterman, R.N.R., who also had had much experience with the Merchant Navy and a long record of convoy escort work. His first lieutenant was a New Zealander and one of

1. A small convoy of twenty-four ships altering course by emergency turn.
All ships should have turned together to the new course ordered by the
Commodore. Normally, convoys altered course by wheeling, when the
outer columns increased and the inner columns reduced speed while gradually
forming up on the new course; this was a lengthy process and to avoid
hazards like U-boats, icebergs and other convoys, emergency turns came to
be used.

2(a). This is one of the first type VII U-boats (500 tons), which formed the great majority of the U-boat fleet. Well designed, tough and quick diving, its only disadvantage was the limited endurance which did not allow long periods off the American coast or other distant areas without re-fuelling.

2(b). The type IX U-boat and its variants were built in smaller numbers. They were larger and less handy than the type VII. This vessel, *U541* (type IXD1), is surrendering at Gibraltar at the war's end. The powerful A.A. guns should be noted.

the other officers is today the Lord Mayor of Westminster. The *Snowflake* was an efficient ship and always ready for anything.

The only ship in the group which had not reached the high standards required was the *Loosestrife* (K105), whose commander was too old for the job, although a fine seaman. His grasp of the problems of a convoy escort was poor, and though he would have made a good captain of an ocean tug or a salvage ship, he was entirely unsuited to an escort, and after this passage, he was to be relieved of his command. In a couple of weeks, the *Loosestrife* had attained the group's standards; but that is another story which, however, illustrates the great influence of the captain of a warship and the importance of getting the right man in the right job.

It will be seen that the group was blessed, with this one exception, with a remarkably good team of commanding officers who were responsible for well-run and efficient ships. Their subsequent careers have borne out the promise of those wartime days.

One serious deficiency worried the escort commander of HX231: the lack of a special rescue ship or even of a trawler or tug which could be used in this role. If a ship were torpedoed, it would be necessary either to leave her to her fate or to detach an escort to pick up survivors, thus further weakening a screen which was already too small to carry out its task fully. Operational research had shown that eight ships were the absolute minimum for a convoy escort group, and to set out with only six, with no rescue ship, swayed the balance of advantage firmly in favour of the U-boats.

All six ships of the group were fitted with the new standard escort equipment. They had a modern asdic set which, after detecting a U-boat, could direct either the dropping of depth-charges from the stern or the throwing of 'Hedgehog' projectiles from the bow

Destroyers and frigates were lively enough at sea, but the corvettes produced something like perpetual motion and it was often said that they would roll in an enclosed dock if left unsecured. In the Atlantic, they rolled and pitched incessantly, and the ships' companies were under great strain. Both the officers and the crews' quarters were small and crowded and meals at sea were a constant struggle, first to prevent the food from sliding off the tables and second, to keep it down once it had been consumed.

All the officers in the corvettes came from the reserves, some from the merchant service (R.N.R.) and the majority from civil life (R.N.V.R.). Of the ship's company, the senior ratings came from the regular Navy, but the great majority of the remainder was 'hostilities only', with only a short training. The senior chief petty officer in the engine-room had the most responsible job of all on the lower deck, for there was no engineer officer and he had full charge of the engines and boilers. The coxswain too had an important task as leader of the lower deck.

The reservists and the 'hostilities only' men learnt quickly in war and were soon equal members of the Royal Navy.

While destroyers and frigates carried a doctor aboard, the corvettes had none, and this meant that the first lieutenant, assisted by a sick-berth attendant, had to deal with medical matters. His duties were light except when survivors were brought on board, at which time a trained doctor was urgently needed.

The absence of a trained doctor also meant that there was no one to do the cipher work, which had to be carried out by watch-keeping officers when off watch. In small ships with a healthy crew, the doctors had little to do except in emergency, but they were usually also ready to help not only with the cipher work but also with the censoring of mail as a way of passing the time.

It is not possible to follow the battle against the U-boats without some understanding of the Allied detection system and of the principal anti-submarine weapons. The paragraphs which follow will attempt to explain the system without recourse to technical jargon.

The asdic set in the escort vessel transmitted a sound wave which passed through the water and hit the target, the echo from which bounced back to the receiver. It was thus possible to measure the range of the target and to determine the bearing of its centre. In addition, a skilful operator by 'training on and off' the target could estimate its approximate size and thus confirm whether it could be a submarine.

For it should be reiterated that, unfortunately, the asdic beam produced echoes, not only of submarines and the hulls of surface ships, but also of fish, of disturbances in the water, of tide rips and even of the wakes of ships and submarines. Identification was a very difficult art and depended much on the skill of the asdic team, which consisted of the control officer, the first operator, who at action stations would be the best operator in the ship, and the second operator. The aids to identification were the sound of the echo – and here experience was all important – the extent of the target, and its movement in bearing. The doppler effect too was important, being a change of pitch of the echo when the target was moving either away from or towards the transmitting ship, which could be detected by the trained ear. A disadvantage was that in bad water conditions when there were layers of water at different temperatures, the asdic beam might be bent and miss the target altogether.

The asdic beam itself was transmitted in the form of a cone from a dome which stuck out of the bottom of the ship, about one-third of the length from the bows. A destroyer with its high speed could 'house' the dome when necessary to avoid damage; frigates and corvettes were slow ships with fixed domes which had to be treated with care, and speed had to be reduced when steaming into a heavy sea.

There was a maximum operating speed of about 18 knots. Above that speed the water noises masked the echoes, and the best operating speed was some 15 knots.

Let us take an imaginary contact. The operator would be sweeping his transmitter from one beam to right ahead and then from the other beam to ahead again. Suddenly he hears an echo (or ping), which sounds like a submarine; and he makes a report. He will be told to 'investigate'; and he then cuts off and on the target to establish its extent. Soon he has estimated the doppler as 'opening', i.e. moving away; the extent of target as 5°, and the movement of the target as 'slowly right'. He classifies the target as submarine and all weapons are brought to the ready. The senior

41

operator probably now takes over the set; and the captain will have pointed the ship to just to the right of the target and increased speed if necessary.

By now the plotting table just below the bridge should have been able to give an estimate of the target's course and speed and all seems to be set for a good attack; the depth-charges are ready and everybody on their toes. The first detection range was 2,100 yards and conditions were good; the target was held firmly until suddenly at 300 yards the operator reported 'no echoes'. This probably meant that the submarine was deep and had got out of the cone of asdic transmission. The attack continued, but there were no echoes to mark the chemical recorder which should give an accurate time for firing the depth-charges. These were therefore dropped in an approximate position determined by a combination of plotting table and stop watch.

During the 'dead time' between losing contact and dropping depth-charges, which themselves fall slowly through the water, the U-boat has had time to take avoiding action and the attack is almost certain to be inaccurate, despite the fact that the depth-charges' settings were changed to a greater depth before firing.

This account of a depth-charge attack on a deep submarine should explain the advantages of the 'Hedgehog' weapon which had been recently fitted to all escorts. It was fitted forward and fired twenty-four quick-sinking projectiles over 100 yards ahead of the ship in a circular pattern. By throwing the projectiles ahead rather than dropping the depth-charges astern, the 'dead time' was much reduced: this gave the U-boat less chance to evade and also caught the deep submarine.

Except in a heavy sea, the 'Hedgehog' was an accurate weapon; and because it was fitted with a contact fuse, it had the advantage that the attacker knew that if he heard an explosion, the U-boat had been sunk. The only disadvantage was that there was no noise if the attack missed, and the U-boat did not have to endure the moral effects of an explosion such as always occurred with depth-charges. The use of the 'Hedgehog' was something of a cat-and-mouse battle and the approach speed of the escort was slow and deliberate.

The ideal team for attacking U-boats was two or even three ships, each attacking in turn, and each keeping a careful eye on the submarine's movements and exchanging information. This was fine when there was known to be only one U-boat present, but in the grim circumstances of a wolf-pack as the opposition there was never any possibility of sending more than one ship of the close escort to hunt a U-boat.

With a support group available, however, it might be possible to leave two ships to hunt a U-boat to destruction.

The depth-charges were similar to those in use for many years, except that they were filled with a new and more effective explosive, 'Torpex.' They would be set to explode at any depth between 50 and 500 feet, but depth estimation was one of the most difficult aspects of attacking submarines and the methods used were primitive. It was better to drop depth-charges at high speed in order to avoid damage to the firing ship, and this was liable to disturb the asdic reception.

For detecting U-boats at night on the surface, each ship was fitted with the new, Type 271 radar, working on the 10 cm. band, which gave excellent discrimination of target. A surfaced submarine could be picked up at some 8,000 yards in good weather; in a flat calm it was sometimes possible to detect a periscope at short range, while a merchant ship could be seen at ranges of some ten miles.

All ships of the group had at least one 4-in. gun, one 2-pdr. pompom and two 20-mm. Oerlikons, all of which could be used against U-boats. Methods of control were liable to be somewhat rudimentary, but the range of such actions was likely to be short, and much could be left to individual gunlayers.

The only H/F D/F set, fitted in the *Tay*, was rather elderly compared with the new set being installed in the *Duncan* during her refit and there was no cathode-ray tube to assist estimation of bearings. But the set was to be invaluable, and as the operators gained experience, they were able to estimate whether the transmitting U-boat was lying in the 'ground ray', which meant within some twenty-five miles, or whether the signals were from the sky wave, when the range was much greater.

The H/F D/F officer had acquired the knack of guessing which of the various wavelengths the U-boats would use when transmitting, and one ship of the convoy, the *Erin*, No. 61, was fitted with a high-frequency receiver and had trained radio officers, so that by asking the *Erin* to listen out on the waves not covered in the *Tay*, it was hoped not to miss an enemy transmission.

For communication between ships of the group, for talking to the commodore, the *Erin* and to escorting aircraft, a radio telephone was used, permanently tuned to 2,410 Kcs.: the convoy wave. In emergency, plain language could be used; but normally all signals were sent either in a simple substitution code, or three-lettered groups or code words were used of which there were many, specially designed for convoy escort work.

Perhaps the main secret of an escort group's success was quick and accurate communication and much care and many exercises were devoted to the tuning of the sets and the alertness of the operators which were to bear fruit when battle was joined. There was some worry in case the U-boats listened to convoy wave or even that they might take bearings of its signals; but it is now known that the U-boats were never fitted with a direction finder which could cover convoy wave and that, except in special experimental boats, they did not listen in to the chatter. The rather indiscriminate use of the wave, which was frowned on by the signal specialists who constantly complained of the group's loquacity, has been shown, therefore, to have been fully justified. Quick communication is almost always preferable to complete security.

In general, B7 Group was well equipped with modern gear and the ships were well trained, though disappointed that so far in the re-formed group's history, the worst enemy had been the weather.

The group was becoming expert, for instance, in 'heaving to' convoys in Atlantic gales – a skilled matter if the ships were not to scatter to the far corners of the ocean – and the escort commander had evolved a 'drill' for 'heaving to' which worked well.

44

But they had not yet been tested out by a major pack attack, and everyone must have had a sneaking worry that, when the time of trial came, they would be found wanting. There was considerable tension in the ships, as the laws of averages indicated clearly that an attack must come soon. Moreover, the Admiralty signals giving the estimated positions of U-boats showed that there were plenty at sea, and it was also known that the preceding HX convoy, HX230, had been sighted and attacked.

Finally, having had a look at the surface escorts, we should consider the aircraft which would give air cover to convoy HX231. Far and away the most important was the American-built Liberator, which had four engines, a patrol endurance of fifteen to sixteen hours and a speed of over 200 knots. Some were fitted with the latest radar in the centimetric band (A.S.V. III) and all were well equipped generally. Each carried a good load of depth-charges.

Based on Iceland or Northern Ireland, these aircraft were to revolutionize the whole defence of convoys.

Of the other aircraft which will enter our story in connection with the rescue of survivors as well as the attack on U-boats, there were two types of flying-boat: the first, the American Catalina, which had a long endurance but a rather slow speed of 150 knots; the other, the British Sunderland, which had given good service, but was now too slow and of too short endurance.

The Flying Fortress was a well-known American heavy bomber. Some of these had been converted for work over the sea. With four engines, it was modern, and nearly as fast as the Liberator, but the endurance on patrol was less.

These aircraft were based mainly in Northern Ireland and Scotland. The flying-boat base at Castle Archdale on Lough Erne in County Fermanagh, for instance, gave excellent service throughout the war.

The task of Coastal Command aircraft over the Atlantic was not easy. There were no electronic aids to navigation in those days, and the aircraft had to rely on dead reckoning and on astronomical methods to find their position. The convoys, because of bad weather, were often far from their reported positions, and in the first years of the war, many aircraft failed to find the convoys which they were due to escort.

The chances of survival if an aircraft were shot down in the Atlantic or had to ditch through engine trouble were very small, though the four engines of most aircraft made the accident-rate low. There was, particularly in winter, the possibility of the weather's deteriorating sharply while the aircraft were on patrol, and making landing hazardous. It was not unusual, for example, for Liberators to take off from Iceland and find themselves landing in Northern Ireland and vice versa.

In order to solve the problem of finding convoys, a system of homing aircraft had been instituted by early 1943. The aircraft would transmit signals on an agreed medium frequency at a pre-arranged time, and a ship of the escort would take a bearing and signal it to the aircraft, using a high frequency. The aircraft would then fly in on the bearing and if all went well there could be no difficulties in finding the convoy. U-boats were fitted with a medium-frequency direction finding set, which was the reason why the escorts made their replies on high frequency: this could not be 'D/F'd except by a German shore station. It did not matter if the U-boats got bearings of the aircraft for they did not transmit when near the convoy.

As soon as the aircraft sighted the convoy, communication was established on convoy wave, and it would pass a message indicating how long it could stay with the convoy: e.g. REM 5 meant that the aircraft could stay for five hours. The escort commanders would then give instructions as to the type of patrol which seemed suitable to the circumstances.

There had been a considerable and understandable reluctance by Coastal Command to place their aircraft under the operational control of the escort commander: a man from another service who they feared might not understand the aircraft's problems. But the decision was correct. The escort commander knew what the situation was on the spot. He knew where the U-boats were likely to be found and what the movements of the convoy would be. No one else was capable of directing the activities of the escorting aircraft, and the system worked well once joint exercises had been started and once mutual confidence between the sailors and the airmen had been established.

The essence of the problem was communication, both mental and physical. In the early days, both had been poor. The two services did not understand each other's problems and seemed to speak a different language; and the number of failures to get into touch by radio were far too frequent. By the spring of 1943, things were improving.

One squadron of Liberators, 120 Squadron, was becoming experienced in the use of the V.L.R. Liberators, which they had been flying for some months. Based in Iceland, they were also becoming accustomed to the problems of convoy escort and had given cover at greater distances than ever before.

Another squadron, 86 Squadron had just converted to these excellent aircraft. It was stationed at Aldergrove in Northern Ireland, and the aircrew were able to visit Londonderry for discussions with their opposite numbers in the escorts. It was also possible for aircraft from 86 Squadron to join in exercises off the River Foyle and for naval officers to fly and so help to bring mutual understanding. Some aircrew, too, came to sea for exercises. Thus, although it was newly converted to the Liberator, 86 Squadron soon picked up the high standards of 120 Squadron, and it was to give excellent service to convoy HX231.

In the next chapter, we return to the convoy which we find formed up and ready for action.

# 4

# The Convoy is Sighted

During the two days after B7 Group joined, little of interest occurred to disturb the peace of the convoy except that the weather improved and with it came an unwelcome increase in the visibility.

The convoy's course was about 025°, which the reader may consider rather more to the north than might be expected. But the object was to get inside the radius of action of the Iceland-based aircraft as soon as possible and for as long as possible. The planners had always to choose between lengthening the passage by diversion towards Iceland and shortening the trip at the expense of the air cover.

On 31 March, the *Vidette* topped up with fuel from the escort tanker, *British Ardour*, and did the same on 3 April, when the *Tay* and the *Pink* also fuelled. The ships were not well versed in the art of fuelling at sea and there were serious delays and some damage to the tanker's equipment.

The tanker first veered astern a light 'grass' steadying line which floated on the water. This was picked up right forward in the bows of the escort and was used to assist station-keeping and to steady the ship being fuelled. It was not used as a towing line. As soon as the grass rope had been secured, the tanker let out the rubber hose which was also buoyant. The escort picked this up with a grappling iron and hauled it inboard through a fair-lead. The end was joined to the connection piece on the forecastle. This was a comparatively simple matter in good weather, but if the sea was rough, it might take a long time, station-keeping was difficult and there was danger of parting both the steadying line and the hose. Much depended on smart drill and skilled ship handling, and training was important. In bad weather, the men working in the bows of the escort got very wet and were in considerable danger.

The *Vidette* fuelled with a following sea running and found station-keeping difficult. On the second 'top up', the hose parted after 130 tons had been received, due to overmuch bight in the hose: in other words, either the steadying line was too short or too much hose had been veered.

It was the *Tay*'s first attempt and in his report the captain modestly remarks that the drill was bad and the station-keeping poor, both due to inexperience. Seventy-three tons were received. Only the *Pink* had no trouble, reporting that the tanker's drill was good, and receiving seventy-four tons of oil. It was satisfactory to have 'topped up' the *Vidette* and the *Tay* before reaching the critical area, for they were faster than the corvettes and it was speed which used up the fuel so quickly.

During the first three days after B7 Group took over, there was no air escort, so one corvette was kept well ahead of the convoy during the day to try to prevent a sighting. Every evening, the *Vidette* was sent on a sweep astern to make sure that no submarines were following the convoy. She had always to be back in station before dark.

The Admiralty situation report was carefully studied but revealed little. We now know that the Tracking Room was 'blind' and unable to pin down the position of the 100 or so U-boats which were at sea. It was just as well that the escorts did not realize that Dönitz knew their position, course and speed, and was about to line up some fifteen U-boats to intercept them!

At midday on 3 April, the Admiralty ordered a small alteration of course which slightly shortened the route. They probably realized that the convoy could not avoid being sighted by U-boats and wanted to reduce the length of time spent in the danger zone. The alteration also facilitated a junction with a conveniently placed support group, consisting of the destroyers *Inglefield, Eclipse, Fury* and *Icarus*, which were refuelling in Iceland.

In anticipation of trouble, the Commander-in-Chief Western Approaches, who was in close touch with the Admiralty Tracking Room, had already asked the British Admiral in Iceland to sail the support group to join convoy HX231 in a position south-west of Iceland as soon as possible. The signal was sent at 0817 (+2) on 3 April, and was a farseeing move. Unfortunately, the weather *en route* was so bad that the support group was unable to arrive until three days later, so for the moment, we must forget these four ships and concentrate on the convoy.

At 1315, 3 April, the *Tay*'s H/F D/F office heard the German shore station (or Control) acknowledging a signal, but nothing was heard of the transmission which was being acknowledged. Shortly after, the Canadian naval headquarters identified it as probably being a sighting report of a convoy in the North-West Atlantic. The approximate position of the U-boat which had made the signal had been fixed by 'poor' D/F as 52° 30 N and 40° W, which was not far from HX231. The signal consisted of forty groups of cipher which could not be decrypted, so it was not known for certain whether HX231 had been seen or not. The reason why the *Tay* did not hear the signal was that it might have been sent from a mysterious zone called the 'skip distance', the name of which is self explanatory.

Anyhow, there were other indications of weak signals both to the west and the east of the convoy, so both the *Tay* and the *Vidette* were sent off on sweeps in likely directions in order to keep the submarines' heads down. They saw nothing, however.

The group was alerted and there was some excitement at the thought of the first battle, but no more signals were heard that night. Although it is now clear that the convoy had not then been sighted, the escort commander firmly believed that a U-boat had reported them, and he and his captains spent an anxious night, as did the ships of the convoy which had been warned that submarines were in the vicinity.

During the night of 3/4 April, a signal was received saying that three Liberators of 120 Squadron R.A.F. would be leaving Newfoundland for Iceland next day at dawn, and would spend some time with the convoy *en route*. This was cheering news to a rather anxious team of escorts, but the weather in Newfoundland proved so bad that none of the aircraft was able to take off and so the convoy was left with no air cover at a time when it was just approaching the enemy patrol line.

As previously mentioned, the endurance of these Liberators was fifteen to sixteen hours, compared with the ten to eleven hours of the Flying Fortress and the eight to nine hours of the Sunderland flying-boat; and they were also faster. On 4 April, there were six Liberators of 120 Squadron serviceable at Reykjavik, and two of them flew an escort for convoy ON176 without incident. HX231 was over 700 miles from base, and presumably at this range it was not considered worth while sending out an aircraft, especially as the three coming from Newfoundland should have helped. This absence of air cover on 4 April was to have serious results.

Let us now look at the German side of the picture. By 31 March, the attack on convoy HX230, which was the one before HX231, had been called off. There had been some slight success, but the U-boat headquarters was disappointed with the results. Only one 'Milch Cow', the *U463*, was at sea and one boat could not provide fuel for all the submarines which needed it. So several were ordered to return to harbour, while the *U463* prepared to fuel sixteen boats.

This left only a comparatively small number of submarines available for the next operation, but at noon on 1 April, the headquarters ordered the formation of a new group to be called *Löwenherz* (Lionheart), with the task of intercepting the next east-bound convoy which happened to be HX231, and whose position, course and speed were known to the cryptographers.

Fifteen boats* were ordered to form the group, some of them coming from HX230 and others from the Bay of Biscay ports. They were to form a patrol on a line of bearing running 350°. The length of the line was 280 miles. The distance apart of boats on the patrol line was only twenty miles so that the convoy ought to be easily intercepted.

The northern end of the line was in position (see map) at 0001 on 3 April and the whole line was instructed to move at 4 knots on a course of 260°. On 2 April, headquarters heard news of the loss of the *U169*, which had been ordered to form part of the group, and the line was adjusted to fill the gap.

On 4 April, headquarters appreciated, correctly, that convoy HX231 was sailing farther to the north than had been expected

* Numbers given in order from south to north: *U169, U191, U168, U630, U635, U706, U260, U564, U592, U572, U530, U563, U594, U584* and *U632*.

and the whole line was ordered to steer 350° at 5 knots: i.e. displace the line together to the north, in order to be certain to catch the convoy; but at 0925, just before this movement had been ordered to be carried out, *U530* (Kapitänleutnant* Lange), which was the fifth boat from the northern end of the patrol line, sighted the convoy and reported its position. Headquarters at once rebroadcast the position to the group as a whole and urged all boats to press home an attack. The *U530* was told to take the role of contact keeper and not to attack until another boat has made contact. Six more U-boats† were ordered to join the *Löwenherz* group if their fuel state permitted, making a total of twenty concentrated on the convoy; and next morning the *U532* was also told to join.

Before dusk, another long signal was sent to the U-boat group, explaining that experience had shown that the night was best, as the escort would be caught off guard and the element of surprise exploited. The U-boats were urged to attack that night, 4 April, and it was made clear that all preparations had been carried out ashore and that it was up to them to gain a great victory.

These long signals of encouragement and admonition ring strangely in British ears. Most of the dispositions should have been standard doctrine and a British admiral would have been content to make them and leave the rest to the men on the spot. But this German practice continued until the end of the war and may have been partly responsible for the astonishingly high morale maintained to the last, despite appalling losses of U-boats. This may well illustrate some of the differences between the German and British characters. The British are not used to being harangued by their commanders and Nelson's famous 'England Expects' signal at Trafalgar was received with a good deal of suspicion. 'Does he expect us *not* to do our duty?' was a typical comment. But Germans evidently appreciate a commander who calls upon them to press on to victory.

Before returning to convoy HX231, we should have a look at the

* Lieutenant-Commander.
† *U229, U415, U134, U598, U306* and *U361*.

U-boats which were to conduct the attack and note their most important characteristics. They all belonged to the Type VII class, of which the majority of U-boats were built. The tonnage was a little over 500 tons, the length was 220 feet, and the complement about forty officers and men.

The maximum speed on the surface was 18 knots which was greater than that of the corvettes in the escort, and the maximum submerged speed was 7 knots. But this submerged speed could be maintained for short bursts only, because of the run-down of the electric battery. The average patrol endurance was estimated to be about 7,000 miles, but endurance figures are almost meaningless as so much depends on the speed at which patrols were carried out. The important fact to note is that the Type VII could remain at sea on a normal patrol for seven or eight weeks without fuelling.

They carried one 88-mm. gun for use against ships and one 20-mm. against aircraft, but the main armament was of course the torpedo. There were four torpedo tubes in the bows and one in the stern, and nine spare torpedoes were carried, making fourteen in all. The control gear was well designed and efficient. The bearing of the target was automatically transmitted from the periscope to the calculator and an estimate of the target speed was added. A firing course was then automatically set in the torpedo and it was thus unnecessary to point the submarine at the target.

For long-range shots, an air-driven torpedo was used, and for the remainder an electric torpedo. Most of the fuses of the warhead were actuated by the magnetism of the target as the torpedo passed underneath, but it was possible to fit an impact fuse and to fix the depth setting to run to hit.

As we have seen, the boats were fitted with a radar search-receiver which gave a warning when metre-length radar waves were being transmitted towards it. But no receiver for centimetric waves had been designed and in the last few months, several boats had been surprised and sunk on the surface.

The U-boats were fitted with excellent hydrophones which 'listened' for propeller noises and could give accurate bearings of the target. When dived to about 100 feet, the hydrophones gave remarkable results, detecting convoys and large warships at ranges of up to fifty miles when the weather and water conditions were suitable. They were little use on the surface, however, so a U-boat shadowing a convoy from outside visibility distances would have to dive from time to time to get a bearing. Unlike British submarines, the U-boats were not fitted with an active sound transmitter so they were unable to get ranges of their targets.

By April 1943, all U-boats were fitted with a device called 'Bold'; this was emitted from a stern tube, forming a large air-bubble which acted as a decoy for the enemy asdic. The British were aware of its existence and it was possible to identify the bubble because of its lack of motion, but this process took some time, and several U-boats had used it successfully to evade their attackers.

All in all, the U-boats were well designed and built. They handled well and dived quickly. They were planned to withstand the pressure at a depth of 600 feet and several had dived even deeper without damage. With their low silhouettes, they were ideally suited to their task.

Of the twenty-one boats which were detailed to attack convoy HX231, there were no names then well known in the U-boat world. By then, most of the commanding officers were inexperienced and of the first wave of U-boat captains, men like Prien, Endrass, Schepke and Kretchmer were either dead, prisoners, or taking a well-earned respite ashore. The junior officers did not have many cruises to their credit and the crews included a number of youngsters on their first operation. There was no lack of volunteers, however, despite the rigours of life in a U-boat and the considerable risk of being sunk.

In December 1942, five U-boats had been sunk; in January 1943, six; in February, nineteen; and in March, fifteen. But although news of the losses spread quickly around the U-boat service, morale remained very high. There were signs, however, that the dilution of experienced officers and men was leading to a drop in efficiency, though this was not yet apparent to the escorts of HX231.

Now we will leave Group *Löwenherz*, steering at best speed for the

3(a). The *Alisma*: the 'Flower' class corvette was the workhorse of the convoy escort force. Handy and seaworthy with a long endurance, the main failing of these ships was the low speed of sixteen knots. Of 259 corvettes built in the U.K. and Canada, thirty-three were lost during the war, mostly by torpedoing.

3(b). The *Tay*: the 'River' class frigate followed the corvette and was larger, and faster with a speed of twenty knots. One hundred and thirty-eight of this class were built in the U.K., Canada and Australia, and nine were lost, all torpedoed. The type 271 radar can be seen above the bridge, and the H/F D/F mast is at the break of the forecastle deck.

4(a). The *Vidette*. Built in 1918, this fine old ship was converted from destroyer to long range escort in 1942. She ran steadily throughout the war and was finally scrapped in 1947. Of the twenty-two ships which were converted, three were lost.

4(b). The *Inglefield*. This destroyer, shown riding a full gale, was built in 1937 as leader of the 'I' class of nine ships. She served mainly with the Home and Mediterranean Fleets and was used only occasionally for convoy work. The *Inglefield* was sunk by bombing in 1944 and only three of the nine ships in the flotilla survived the war.

convoy reported by *U530* at 0924, and later by U630, on 4 April, and return to B7 Escort Group.

*U530*'s first sighting report had been intercepted in the *Tay*'s H/F D/F office which estimated the bearing of *U530* as 285°; the signal was in the 'ground-wave' and was therefore close. Several other signals were received from that direction, which was on the port beam of the convoy which was steering 025°, so the *Vidette* was sent out to investigate. She failed to see any submarines, but the *U530* reports having been forced to dive by an escort at about this time, so *Vidette*'s journey was not wasted.

It is now clear from the position of the sighting submarine that the convoy had in fact passed through the patrol line undetected during the night. *U530*, however, caught a sight of the ships just after dawn: to the eastwards. Passing through the line was an advantage to the convoy as the U-boats would now have to pursue from astern rather than home in from ahead as usually happened when a convoy blundered into a patrol line.

However, it did not take long for *U572* (Oberleutnant* Kummetat) at 1148 and *U363* (Kplt Hartmann) at 1243 to sight and report; and the *Tay*'s H/F D/F office was kept very busy taking bearings of the ground-wave signals which came streaming in. *U530* reports having been forced to dive again by an escort at 1200, as does *U572* at 1419, so although the ships concerned had no idea of the presence of the submarines, their routine sweeps and zigzags were having a good effect.

Then at 1451, a strong signal was received on 238° – the port quarter of the convoy – and the *Vidette*, which was stationed astern, was sent out again on the bearing. She sighted a conning-tower fifty minutes later, reported the fact on convoy wave and all concerned now knew that the radio signals had been confirmed by a physical sighting, that the crunch had come, and that the convoy was in for a big battle.

The submarine which the *Vidette* had seen was the *U594* and when first sighted was eight miles away, to the south-west. In order to avoid alerting the U-boat, the *Vidette* did not alter course at once to point at it, but held on. The submarine was

* Lieutenant.

estimated to be steering 045°, which was towards the convoy, but it soon altered away and it was clear that it was taking avoiding action. At 1630, the *Vidette* got a range, for the first time by radar, of 6,000 yards on a bearing of 190° and the submarine steered 170°. *Vidette* still avoided pointing straight at the U-boat, but increased to 22 knots which was the best speed in the prevailing weather conditions. By 1637, the U-boat was bearing 142° at a range of 5,800 yards, and five minutes later, it dived. The *Vidette* steered for the diving position, reduced to 18 knots, which was the maximum speed at which asdics could be operated effectively, and hoped for the best. Unfortunately, no trace of the submarine was heard, so a five-charge, depth-charge pattern was dropped on the estimated diving position, set to explode at 100 feet. Speed was then further reduced to 16 knots and a deliberate search in the form of a square box was started.

At 1718, at the start of the third leg of the box, an asdic echo was reported and two minutes later, it was classified as 'submarine', with a range of 1,500 yards. The depth-charges were brought to the ready and the 'Hedgehog, was told to stand by, but because the firing course was almost directly into the sea and swell, and there was much motion on the ship, it was decided to drop depth-charges. Just before firing, the target appeared to alter rapidly, and the *Vidette* 'threw off' to allow for the move. Fourteen depth-charges were dropped when the recorder trace reached the correct position, set to depths between 150 and 300 feet. It was judged to be an accurate attack and the German records confirm, for *U594* reports having been 'effectively depth-charged'. Damage was caused to electrical gear, a valve in the hull was fractured and water started to flow into the boat, but the situation was controlled by competent repair crews.

The *Vidette* regained contact with the submarine soon after the attack and prepared to go in again. At 1727, 'no echoes' was reported, but three minutes later, the U-boat was picked up again. As the wind and sea were now astern, it was decided to try the 'Hedgehog'. Speed was reduced to 9 knots and the destroyer crept quietly towards the target.

Unhappily, the 'Hedgehog' pattern missed and, soon after,

contact with *U594* was lost. Before another search could be started, the ship was ordered by the escort commander to break off and course was set to rejoin the convoy at 22 knots. The captain of *U594* was a lucky man as the 'Hedgehog' pattern cannot have missed by much, and another attack would probably have been fatal.

In his report, Lieutenant Hart, the *Vidette*'s captain, says that he did not open fire on the submarine because it presented such a small target and he wanted it to stay on the surface until the last moment. Commodore Simpson, the senior officer at London-derry, in his comments, suggests that *Vidette* acted astutely in not pointing directly at the U-boat and in not opening fire, but he considered that once within 6,000 yards, the U-boat should have been approached directly at best speed, so as to save time in getting contact after it dived.

Despite the criticism, the *Vidette* executed a very good attack and the assessment of the Admiralty U-boat Committee as 'probably damaged' was most accurate. The *U594* was badly shaken and repairs took some time.

In his report, the escort commander remarks that the U-boat tried to draw the *Vidette* away from the convoy and that the effort was successful. When the first of the night attacks came, however, the *Vidette* was only two miles astern of the convoy, although her appearance did have unfortunate consequences as we saw earlier.

Meanwhile, there had been much other activity. The *Alisma*, already on an extended screen ahead of the convoy, was sent out on an H/F D/F bearing of 350° at 1617 and quickly sighted a submarine, which promptly dived. This was probably *U563* which reports having been harried by an escort at about this time.

*U572* was also busy and reports that after having been forced to dive by an escort at 1419, he continued to approach the convoy while submerged. Kummetat cannot have been very skilled and certainly did not use his periscope enough, for at 1507, he was rammed by one of the merchant ships of the convoy! The bows were damaged and a torpedo tube was put out of action. It is extraordinary that no report of any bump was received from any ship of the convoy, and we will never know which one did the damage. Probably the weather was such that the bumping of the hull in the heavy seas prevented the ramming from being felt on board.

Next, at 1817, the *Tay*'s look-out sighted a submarine on the horizon ahead of the convoy. The *Tay*, which was on the starboard bow, belted out at best speed until it dived. This was *U229* which had just made its sighting report. The *Tay* did not have time to start a hunt, but had to return to the convoy to ward off the next attempt.

The situation now appeared rather grim. Three U-boats had been sighted and it was known from the signalling that several others were around. Actually *U530*, *U572*, *U563*, *U594* and *U229* had all made firm contact and other boats were close.

The escorts were disappointed that they had not done more to prevent the assembly of the pack, but in fact, it was only aircraft which could have been successful in stopping it. A look at the German records shows that the escorts did better than they realized at the time, and the position would certainly have been worse if they had not been so active. And, of course, they had no idea that one of the enemy had been rammed in the convoy.

The picture was one of the perfect prologue of a classic pack attack on a large scale. The convoy had passed through the patrol line, fourteen submarines were in reach and six others had been ordered to join. The deliberate assembly of the pack had taken place in excellent visibility, unhampered by air cover. Admiral Dönitz must have felt pleased that evening, and must have expected great news next day.

It was a remarkable coincidence that as the escorts waited tensely for the next attack, in each ship a cipher message from Admiral Horton was being decoded.

It was addressed to all the ships in the Western Approaches Command and read:

> 'I congratulate the officers and men of the Western Approaches Escort Force, of the U.S.N. and R.C.N. groups working with us, on the splendid work successfully carried out in guarding and maintaining all our sea-borne communtations during this, the most violent and tempestuous

winter for many years. I appreciate the short lay-overs and the prolonged voyages due to weather and diversions imposed on you, and I recognize to the full your endurance and devotion which enabled the essential dates to be kept despite every hardship and difficulty and with such unfailing cheerfulness.

'With the spring come welcome reinforcements and besides there is reason to believe that the convoy programme may settle down and allow reasonable periods in harbour. With better weather and longer lay-overs we must concentrate on working up individual ships to group efficiency and to establish a 100 per cent kill-rate for every U-boat located.

'With the extra escorts and aircraft, together with the improved training facilities, it will be only necessary for each ship to reach the 100 per cent killing standard for the situation in the Atlantic to turn radically in our favour.

'Nothing will dishearten the Hun more than to know that the Battle of the Atlantic has been lost, when it is his last hope of defeating Britain.'

Here was rare praise for past work and encouragement for the future. It was addressed of course to the whole Command, and not just to B7 Group, but it provided a pleasant feeling that the efforts of the past three months had been appreciated, and it gave confidence for the night ahead.

# 5

# The First Night's Attacks

Let us now for the sake of clarity review briefly the events during the first attack of the night which have been already outlined at length in Chapter 1.

As the wind was strong from the port beam of the convoy, the escort had been strengthened on that side, a decision to do this being then quickly made dubious by the appearance of northern lights after dark. In addition to the gaps on the starboard side, the *Vidette*, which was bound for the stern position, was still four miles away having been delayed by a hunt for a U-boat.

All the equipment was in working order in the escorts, though the weather conditions were likely to reduce the range of detections. The convoy was keeping good station.

Just after dark, the convoy's course had been altered 45° to port, with instructions to the commodore to resume the original course automatically at 2300. It was hoped in this way to confuse the U-boats' attacks.

The first incident of the night had been a false alarm when one of the merchant ships had dropped a bright flare into the water by mistake. It had taken some time to 'douse' the flare and tension in the convoy had increased.

Then at 2208 disaster had struck. A flash was seen by the *Tay*, which after some delay it was decided must have come from a torpedo hitting the *Shillong*, the leading ship of the eleventh column, which was some five miles away from the *Tay*.

The standard search operation 'Half Raspberry' was carried out without effect, probably because of the delay in ordering it. The U-boat responsible, *U630*, escaped undetected.

The *Tay* had been ordered to move from the port to the starboard quarter position in order to try to cut off the escaping U-boat, but was delayed by some unnecessary confusion involving the identification of the *Vidette*, rejoining from astern.

The *Shillong* sank very quickly and the fate of the survivors was tragic.

One further piece of evidence eventually emerged which confirmed the account of what must have happened. When the master of the *Stephen Foster* was interviewed on return to harbour he reported having seen a conning-tower shortly after the torpedoing. His ship was the third in the next column to the *Shillong*. For some unexplained reason he did nothing about it, neither firing at the submarine nor making a report. It was mistakes like this which made the escort's tasks even more difficult.

The illumination was stopped at 2230 and at 2242 the escorts were ordered to take up new stations so as to cover both bows, both beams and the stern position which the *Vidette* had just reached.

Thus far the summary. Now to continue the narrative's progress.

There were now only five escorts on the screen, all waiting for the next attack. There was another false alarm, however, when the *Tay* detected a radar echo on the starboard beam of the convoy, steering to the eastward at 15 knots. She chased the echo, which proved to be a merchant ship which had broken out of the convoy, and other than to signal 'return to convoy', which was ignored, there was nothing for the *Tay* to do than to go back to her station as soon as possible.

Soon after, at 2300, the convoy started to make its prearranged alteration of course to starboard and at 2303, before the *Tay* was back in station, an explosion was heard. At 2307, the escort commander signalled on convoy wave 'another ship torpedoed' and at 2310 the *Waroonga*, the fourth ship in the fourth column, reported coolly back on the same wave that she had been torpedoed on the starboard quarter.

Because the escorts were still not back in station after the last attack, 'Half Rasberry' was not ordered. Some star-shell illumination was laid on but it failed to find the U-boat.

In his report, the escort commander said that he thought that the submarine must have fired from the starboard quarter from 'a position where the *Tay* would have been if she had not been diverted by the ship which broke out, but subsequent analysis shows that this cannot have happened. It seems certain that again the U-boat came in from ahead and passed down between the fourth and fifth columns, torpedoing the *Waroonga* as it passed.

The *Waroonga* soon reported that she was able to maintain convoy course and speed, despite being hit, so that there were no survivors to worry about and all escorts were ordered to regain station in preparation for the next attack.

There seems no doubt that it was the *U635* which torpedoed the *Waroonga*. The captain, Oblt Eckermann, reported later to Control that he attacked the convoy at the approximate time of the hit, and had claimed two merchant ships torpedoed. *U635* was sunk next day, so its log is not available, but the evidence is strong that it gained one success first.

Two other submarines, the *U260* and the *U563* sighted the star-shell and flares fired after the *Waroonga* hit, and both were deterred from pressing home their attacks by the light and by the activity of the escorts, so it is evident that the decision to illuminate after the second attack was correct. It was a delicately balanced problem. To illuminate at once might find the submarine responsible, and would certainly discourage any U-boats following up which would hesitate to enter a well-lit convoy on the surface. But to leave illumination until too late, would merely pinpoint the convoy's position for the benefit of all the U-boats in the area.

Up to now, no ground-wave signals had been received in the H/F D/F office since dark, and therefore no warning of attack had been possible. Presumably, the submarines had made their attack without preliminary signals. Just before midnight, however, some signals which appeared to be close were heard on the port beam and the escorts were warned accordingly.

At 0127 on 5 April, the *Snowflake*, whose station was on the port beam, detected a submarine submerged. It seems probable that this was the *U572* which had been forced to dive by the earlier illumination. On the *Snowflake*'s first attack, the run in towards the target was directly into the sea and swell and a speed of more than 10 knots was not possible. Contact was lost at 300 yards and so the U-boat was fairly deep; no depth-charges were dropped. But the corvette turned round smartly and regained contact, and a good attack was delivered on a course with the sea and swell astern. Nine depth-charges were dropped – there was one misfire – and after the seventh explosion, a long rumbling noise was heard, much louder than the remainder. The charges were set to go off at 150 and at 300 feet.

$U572$, however, reports that he was lying at 360 feet and so the charges were too shallow to cause damage. Lieutenant Chesterman's assessment was that the U-boat had 'been given a severe headache' and this is near the mark for he prevented the boat from surfacing and coming in for another attack. The Admiralty U-boat Committee's estimate was 'insufficient evidence of damage'.

By the end of the second attack, the *Snowflake* was some eight miles astern of the convoy, so she set off to return at best speed, having reported the situation to the escort commander.

In the H/F D/F office, it was estimated from ground-wave signals that several U-boats were now astern of the convoy, out of harm's way; and it was assumed, correctly, that these were boats which had either attacked successfully or been driven off and were reporting accordingly to Control. But one boat was still ahead of the convoy and made several signals. It was possible to follow its progress down the starboard side of the convoy, keeping the escorts informed of its position until it was on the quarter well clear. Again, one assumes that the boat had been kept away by the movements of the *Alisma* and the *Tay*, both alert and watching, but neither of which detected its presence. It was probably the $U168$, which reports having sighted the convoy at about this time but which complained that it was driven off by two escorts. $U706$ also sighted the convoy at about this time but failed to make an attack.

No sooner had this alarm subsided, than another submarine was heard ahead of the convoy by the H/F D/F office. All escorts were warned accordingly, and the *Alisma* immediately picked up a radar contact which she investigated. It soon proved to be a tanker, the *Aruba*, which was trying to break away, but the *Alisma*

63

persuaded her to return to station by what must have been some tough Australian threats and then turned to get back to the convoy. Almost at once, at 0228, she picked up another radar contact. This time it was the *U564*.

The *Alisma*'s contact was at 2,000 yards, and it placed the submarine nearly ahead of the starboard wing column of the convoy: a dangerous position. Radar contact was lost at 1,000 yards, and an asdic contact was gained which might or might not have been the U-boat. A depth-charge pattern was dropped by eye over the position where it was estimated the boat might be, and the *Alisma* turned to get back to her station on the bow to ward off the next attacker. She soon got another radar contact, however, and fired a star-shell in the light of which a conning-tower was sighted. Radar contact was then lost as the U-boat dived. The asdic operator gained a good contact which was held for a short spell, and a ten-charge, depth-charge pattern was fired: this time a stop-watch was used for judging the time to fire, as the recorder had lost contact.

The *U564*'s report shows that the submarine did not in fact dive during the first attack, when the *Alisma* did not fire a star-shell, and the asdic contact must have been a false one. The captain of *U564*, Oblt Fiedler, must have been a very cool customer to risk being rammed by keeping on the surface as he did, to evade the first attack. The second attack, however, was very accurate. A periscope was damaged and No. 3 tank was torn open. Next morning in daylight attempts were made to repair the damage, but they failed and the *U564* had to return to harbour at Lorient.

It might be said that the *Alisma*'s attack was a little lucky, as it was carried out by stop-watch rather than recorder trace, but she had a very good A/S team and they deserved success.

Other than a report from the *Pink* at 0300 that she had failed to find any survivors of the *Shillong*, there was little else to report that night, and all the U-boat signals heard came from the safe directions of astern and on the quarter. The *Pink* was ordered to rejoin and was back in her station by 0900, 5 April.

At 0345, the *Vidette* was told to move from the position astern to the position ahead of the convoy, so as to be ready for a submerged attack at dawn by a submarine which had kept quiet and not revealed its presence. But fortunately, nothing transpired.

At daybreak, it was possible to count the ships and to take stock of the situation. Two ships had been torpedoed, one of which was still remaining with the convoy; and taking into account the size of the German opposition, the results were considered satisfactory. It might have been much worse. The group's efficiency, after the initial delay in reporting the *Shillong* torpedoing, had been good and ships had acted sensibly and not waited for orders.

There was a blacker side to the picture, however, for it was found that three ships had broken out of the convoy during the night, presumably at about 2230 when the *Tay* had been diverted by a ship which refused to return to her station. All three had been in the starboard wing column close to the *Shillong*, and the fact that two had not been detected leaving was because that side had been left thinly defended.

In addition, the American tanker *Sunoil* had suffered engine trouble and was straggling astern of the convoy.

Of the three 'breakers out', the American *Thomas Sumpter* reappeared during the forenoon, safe and sound, and took up her old position; but the Dutch *Blitar* and the Swedish *Vaarlaren* were sunk by U-boats, as was the *Sunoil*. An account of what happened to them will be found in Chapter 10.

The escort commander was not dissatisfied with the group's 'blooding', and the escorts had improved steadily as the night drew on. It is interesting now to read in the German records of the numbers of times when U-boats failed to press home their attacks because of the presence of escorts, zigzagging on the screen and blissfully unaware of a submarine's presence. Hartmann in *U563* remembers the night well and writes that he had difficulty in keeping contact, having to dive several times to listen on hydrophones.

The leader was especially pleased with the work of the H/F D/F office which, except for the first two attacks which had been carried out 'silently', had given good warning of the approach of

U-boats and provided a clear picture of the situation. Its efficiency and confidence had increased as the night drew on.

It was finally concluded that, considering the weather conditions which had been entirely in favour of the enemy, the defence had not done too badly. The escort commander was certainly more confident that things would go better on the next night, and the night after that, if the U-boats continued to keep contact.

It is interesting to read, after thirty years, the remarks of the senior officers on the escort commander's report, which of course was written soon after the convoy arrived in harbour. They agreed in general with the analysis of events which was given and with the attribution of blame. It is surprising, however, that there was no suggestion that the dangers of straggling or, worse still, of deliberate breaking out of convoy should not be brought home to merchant ships. Not only did a 'breaker out' divert the defending escort: it condemned itself to certain suicide.

# 6

## Attacks During The Day of 5 April

After the dawn muster of the convoy between 0500 and 0600, there were several administrative tasks to be carried out. The commodore had to be kept informed of the situation and the commander-in-chief who had been told briefly of the first night attack had to be put fully in the picture. The commodore was informed verbally, the *Tay* going alongside the *Tyndareus* for a brief talk; and a long signal was dispatched to the shore, reporting the events of the night and asking for a tug to be sailed to the help of the torpedoed *Waroonga*.

Shortly after this signal had been sent off, another was received from the commander-in-chief, ordering the convoy to alter course forthwith for a new position on the route. The object of the alteration was given as facilitating the junction with the support group from Iceland, though in a contemporary report to the First Sea Lord, the reason was stated to be because there was likely to be no flying from Iceland that day: a forecast which fortunately proved incorrect. Whatever the reason, the alteration, which involved a turn of 50° to starboard to 090°, did shorten the voyage. The manœuvre took a long time to complete with such a large convoy. The outer columns increased speed, the inner columns decreased speed and gradually they got back into their 'box' formation.

Just as the turn was finished, a signal of distress was received from the *Sunoil*, the straggler, saying that she was being attacked by a submarine. The escort commander sent the *Vidette*, the fastest ship, to her assistance immediately. The visibility was good, but as will be recounted later, the *Vidette* found no trace of the unfortunate tanker and in accordance with her orders rejoined the convoy before dark. However, at 1110, *U168* reported having been forced to dive by an escort, and from the position given this can only have been the *Vidette*, so one shadower was forced to break off contact. While the *Vidette* was away, the *Snowflake* took her place astern of the convoy.

From dawn onwards, a stream of signals in the ground-waves was received in the H/F D/F office, mostly from astern and from the port beam and it was assumed that the U-boats were reporting to Control on the events of the preceding night. In fact, it is now known that Group *Löwenherz* was informed in blunt terms later that morning that radio silence was being broken unnecessarily, especially during daylight, and that convoy positions and reports of sinkings only were important. All boats in contact were urged to get up ahead of the convoy for submerged attack and only the contact keeper had to report before attacking, so that another boat could be detailed to take over that duty. Just after dawn, *U260* (Kplt Purkhold) had taken over as contact keeper, many boats having lost touch during the later part of the night when the escort counter-attacks had been so successful. Five other boats had soon joined *U260* in regaining contact and it was these which must have been responsible for the signals heard in the *Tay*. The visibility is described in the latter's report of proceedings as 'horribly good'.

The escort commander's main preoccupation at this moment, however, was the time of arrival of the first aircraft, the intended programme of which had been signalled during the night. Only by constant air patrols around the perimeter of the convoy could the U-boats be prevented from steaming fast on the surface to gain position for further attacks.

An intensive air plan had been prepared for 5 April, which was intended to give the convoy cover during almost all the day.

First there was to be a Liberator of 86 Squadron, flying from Northern Ireland, which should have joined soon after daybreak. This would be followed by two more Liberators from Iceland, taking off at two hours' interval, whose operations should have covered the rest of the day.

In addition, five Catalina flying-boats of the U.S. Navy, operating from Iceland, were due to fly a parallel track patrol near convoy HX231, while another Liberator from Iceland was due to sweep between convoys HX231 and SC124, which was farther south. It was an ambitious programme, though there was too much emphasis on patrols and sweeps and not enough on close escort. It promised well.

Unfortunately plans did not work out according to programme. Only one Catalina flying-boat, C of 84 Squadron, completed its mission, and the other four had to return to base because of bad weather.

The Liberator on sweep between convoys HX231 and SC124 sighted a periscope between the two, but owing to its height at the time was unable to attack before the periscope disappeared. A search failed to find any trace of the submarine, and it is difficult to determine from the records which U-boat, if any, was involved.

The most important task of all, the provision of air escort, was not going well. The first Liberator due, X of 86 Squadron from Aldergrove, had to return to base owing to bad weather *en route* and did not reach the convoy, which was therefore left unprotected during the vital period between dawn and midday.

There was also trouble in homing on to the convoy the first Liberator from Iceland, P of 120 Squadron. The homing procedure was started at 1000(+2) but the aircraft did not receive the signals from the *Tay* which informed it of its bearing, and it missed the convoy and did not sight it until 1235. The aircraft's radio receiver cannot have been tuned correctly, as no trouble was experienced with Liberator N of 120 Squadron which had taken off later from the same base, but had sighted the convoy at 1145, well before its companion.

Liberator N of 120 Squadron was soon very busy, and the captain, Flying Officer Matherley, sighted a U-boat ten miles on the port beam of the convoy before there had been even time to exchange information with the escort commander and receive patrol instructions.

The aircraft was at 1,000 feet below the cloud base, and the visibility was good. The submarine, which was *U584* (Kplt Deecke) was steering the same course and speed as the convoy – 090° at about 9 knots – and was first sighted on the starboard bow at a range of three miles.

The aircraft turned to starboard and dived at the U-boat,

approaching from the sun and catching it apparently unawares, as the attack was made while the boat was fully surfaced. Six 'Torpex' depth-charges were dropped, spaced at 100 feet apart from a height of only fifty feet. The engineer, watching through the bomb-doors, saw two depth-charges explode close to the conning-tower, while the rear gunner saw four splashes on the track ahead of the boat, which immediately dived.

Three markers were dropped in the position of the attack, but no further sign of the U-boat was seen.

The *U584* had been in contact with the convoy since dawn and was clearly surprised by the attack. Kplt Deecke notes that it was 'close', but does not mention damage. However, he broke off contact and did not take any further part in operations against convoy HX231.

The attack had a further bonus, because the contact keeper, *U260*, reports diving at about this time because of an air attack on a submarine in the near vicinity. *U260* was kept submerged by a series of explosions which it reports coming from both escorts and aircraft.

The U-boat Assessment Committee, having looked at the photographs taken during Flying Officer Matherley's attack on *U584*, described it as 'excellent and accurate' and estimated that the submarine had probably been sunk; but my analysis and that by post-war historians shows that this was somewhat over-optimistic.

A little later, the remaining aircraft of the Catalina patrol, C of 84 Squadron, sighted a submarine to the west of the convoy and made two good attacks. The *U592* reports having been machine-gunned and depth-charged by a flying-boat at about the same time as that given for the Catalina attack, and there seems to be little doubt as to identity. The *U592*'s captain, Kplt Borm, reports slight damage, with a fuel tank leaking inboard, but this was repaired. The U-boat continued to shadow and did not have to break off the operation.

Let us now take up the story of a brave commander, Kplt von Zitzewitz of *U706*, who had been in contact with the convoy from about midnight until 0630 when he lost touch. The *U706* had been on the starboard side of the convoy during the night and was therefore lucky to regain contact at 0952 when von Zitzewitz found himself directly ahead, due undoubtedly to the alteration of course of 50° to starboard at about 0900. But for the alteration, he might have failed to gain touch and would certainly not have been in such a fine position.

At 1012, soon after sighting the convoy, the *U706* also saw the *U584* nearby but the report does not mention whether they exchanged intentions by signal. If they did, it must have been by visual means as no radio signals were received in the H/F D/F office on that bearing.

The *U706* was determined to attack and steered for the convoy, remaining submerged throughout and showing a periscope for as short periods as possible.

The situation in the convoy was that formation had been regained after the alteration of course. The course was 090° at 9 knots and five escorts were present. The *Snowflake* was astern, the *Loosestrife* on the port bow, the *Tay* ahead of the commodore's column in the centre, the *Alisma* on the starboard bow and the *Pink* on the starboard beam. It may well be asked why, with so few escorts, one had to be kept in the stern position where no submerged attack could be expected. The answer was that it was essential to keep the convoy in good order, to chase up stragglers and to keep an eye on the damaged *Waroonga*.

At 1208, the escort commander heard of the attack on the U-boat by N of 120 Squadron which could now be seen on the port beam circling its victim, and on the principle of taking the offensive as quickly as possible, he instructed the *Tay*, which was the fastest ship still present, to go out on the bearing at best speed to help the aircraft.

The *U706* reports passing, at 1152, an escort which was sweeping ahead of the port side of the convoy. This can only have been the *Loosestrife*. A quick look through the periscope showed the *U706* to be ahead of the port-wing column. At least two ships were sighted and the submarine prepared to attack. Then at 1209, an escort, which must have been the *Tay* leaving her station, passed over the submarine which was at a depth of fifty-five feet.

71

As soon as the *Tay* was clear, the *U706* raised its periscope again, sighted a tanker and 'although the angle was not very good' fired two torpedoes. The submarine which was then probably between the fourth and fifth columns, dived deep.

At 1215, one torpedo hit the escort tanker, *British Ardour* (No. 62) which was the second ship in the sixth column. When it struck, there was an enormous explosion, a sheet of flame and a great column of smoke arose in the air. Oil was sprayed all over the foredeck and the bridge which promptly caught fire. The engines were stopped and the crew prepared to abandon ship.

The second torpedo missed the tanker and passed the stern of the *Tyndareus*, the commodore's ship, which was leading the seventh column. This second torpedo's course was reported as 140°, and another ship in the eighth column, the *Port Sydney* (No. 82) also confirms this. It was by then at the end of its run and moving slowly on the surface of the sea. The *Port Sydney* fired machine-guns at the torpedo and claims to have sunk it. The *Tyndareus* and the *Port Sydney*, both fine ships with invaluable cargoes, had had lucky escapes.

Immediately after the explosion in the *British Ardour*, the escort commander had ordered operation 'Artichoke' which was the pre-arranged plan to be carried out when a ship in convoy was torpedoed by day. The ship in the rear position, in this case the *Snowflake*, went straight to the torpedoed ship, investigated the situation and circled the wreck in a search for the U-boat which sometimes remained nearby.

All the other escorts turned outwards to the reciprocal course of the convoy, the ships in front immediately, the remainder delaying their turn so as to form a rough line abreast. They then swept down the path of the convoy, hoping to pick up the U-boat by asdic. But they could find no trace of *U706*.

In the light of knowledge of the U-boat's track, it is clear that water conditions were poor and that the asdics did not produce good results. The *U706* passed close both to the *Loosestrife* and the *Tay* and in normal conditions should have been picked up on the asdics and prevented from firing torpedoes. Subsequent analysis too showed that during operation 'Artichoke', the submarine must have passed within detection range of the *Tay* again. Kplt von Zitzewitz had carried out a bold, determined and successful attack, but he had been lucky. The chances of detection, even in poor conditions, should have been fair as he passed within detection range three times.

In his report of proceedings, the escort commander upbraided himself for a serious error of judgement in starting to leave the escort screen in order to chase after the U-boat which was being attacked on the horizon by the aircraft. He assumed that the submarine had made its attack through the gap left when the *Tay* moved to the northward. It is some small consolation now to know that this move took the *Tay* over the submarine and therefore gave a better chance of detecting it than if no move had been made.

But in principle the decision had been wrong. The convoy was still surrounded, the number of escorts on the screen was very low and to take away one more was asking for trouble. The escort commander excused himself by pleading that he was imbued with the offensive spirit, but he should have known better.

There was however no leisure for these self-analytical thoughts at the time. When the escorts, still carrying out operation 'Artichoke', had reached a position 6,000 yards astern of the convoy, they all turned together to resume their stations. By now it had been established that the *British Ardour* had been hit on the port side, and the chances were strong that the U-boat was still on the port side of the convoy. The return course was then altered 30° to port accordingly to search the port side more thoroughly, but again without any success. In fact the *U706* remained submerged for five hours and escaped undetected.

The *Snowflake* then received instructions, which were to try to persuade the crew of the *British Ardour* to return to their ship and to try to extinguish the fire, as the tanker showed no signs of sinking. A further account of this ordeal will be found later.

Liberator N of 120 Squadron had to be given a patrol – this was done by ordering one of the 'reptile' code words, such as Mamba, Cobra or Adder – and she was requested to fly round the convoy at visibility range in order to try to prevent submarines from staying on the surface.

By about 1330, all four remaining escorts were back in station, with the *Pink* now in the stern position. At the same time, the other Liberator, P of 120 Squadron, which had first missed the convoy, finally arrived and was given a patrol on the port beam where the H/F D/F bearings indicated most activity, and where several U-boats seemed to be shadowing.

The effect of having two aircraft covering the convoy was almost magical. There had been a short burst of signalling between 1328 and 1341, with the bearings coming from all round the convoy.

In each case, an aircraft was sent out on the bearing indicated, and at 1400, *U594* reports having been attacked by four depth-charges. The attack was not accurate and no damage was inflicted, but *U594* had to dive. No report form seems to have been submitted by the aircrew so that it cannot be firmly established which aircraft was responsible, though it seems likely to have been P of 120 Squadron.

After 1341, not one signal was heard in the H/F D/F office until 1721, which was exactly ten minutes after both Liberators had had to leave the convoy owing to shortage of fuel. For four hours therefore, they had imposed complete radio silence on the U-boats, all of which, I think must have submerged to avoid the dreaded dive from the sky and the falling depth-charges.

There was now at least three hours' daylight to survive without air cover, which was a worrying thought. So the escort commander arranged to 'home' an imaginary aircraft. He pretended to establish contact with it, while another escort, the *Loosestrife*, made the missing aircraft signals. There is no evidence that the enemy were listening to the convoy wave, so the ruse was unsuccessful, as was a later plot when the escort commander's night intentions were sent off to ten escorts instead of the five present!

Soon after the two Liberators had left, there was another burst of radio activity from the enemy which showed that the convoy was still surrounded. The lack of an aircraft to fill in the hours before dark had been serious. The position was unpleasant with only four escorts still present: one ahead, one astern and one on each bow. The *Waroonga* was still in need of constant watching, and visibility was good, though the weather showed signs of getting worse.

However, no further attacks came before dark, although *U191* seems to have made contact and tried unsuccessfully to get into position. The unexpected lull gave captains of ships a chance to get a meal and a short rest before sunset when it was necessary to take up night stations again, preparatory to the next wave of attacks.

The day had been disappointing. No survivors from the *Shillong* had been found and it was feared that no one had been rescued. Distress signals had been received from the *Blitar*, some distance away from the convoy, and from the *Sunoil*. The *Vidette* had found no trace of the *Sunoil* and analysis today shows that she must have been well to the north of her estimated position. Nothing had been heard of the *Vaarlaren*.

The loss of the *British Ardour*, the sole remaining tanker capable of refuelling escorts had been a bitter blow, and the failure to detect the submarine which had sunk her had made it worse. It was fortunate that the *Vidette* and the *Tay* had topped up with fuel just before the battle had started. There was no shortage of oil among the corvettes.

There were probably two nights and two days of further battle to endure before the convoy got out of the danger zone into an area where constant air patrols made life most unpleasant for U-boats. Everyone was rather tired, but all were reasonably confident that they could hold their own against the enemy, given normal circumstances.

To consider the bright side, the performance of the two Liberators during their coverage of the convoy had been most encouraging and great hopes were placed on more air cover next day. In addition, the support group of four destroyers from Iceland was due to join next morning and this would bring a welcome increase in strength.

In the light of hindsight, it is clear from the U-boats' reports that the routine zigzags and movements of the escorts continued to keep submarines away from the convoy and that any activity, however pointless it may have seemed at the time, may well have been rewarding.

It is interesting to consider why *U584*, which was ahead of the convoy with *U706* before the latter attacked, did not make any similar effort. If the captain had followed *U706*, he would have found the convoy undefended during operation 'Artichoke'. Perhaps he failed to estimate the course of the convoy correctly and assumed that it was still steering north-east instead of east. For it was *U584* which was attacked by Liberator N of 120 Squadron on the convoy's port beam, just before *U706* torpedoed the *British Ardour*.

# 7

# The Night of 5/6 April

The situation at dusk was very worrying. The weather was in the U-boats' favour, as it was rough enough to reduce the detection range of the radar and also to make the asdic less effective. The night was dark, but clear with no moon.

We know now that there were still twenty submarines operating against the convoy, though by no means all were in contact. *U191* had sighted the convoy at 1856 and at 1945 *U270* had sighted and reported it from ahead, noticing two escorts on the starboard side. Great hopes were raised ashore at the German headquarters of successful attacks during the night: these are reflected in the War Diary entries.

After discussion and thought, the escort commander requested the commodore to alter the course of the convoy 30° to port just after dark and to alter back 40° to starboard three hours later. This was intended to bring the convoy to its rendezvous with the support group soon after daylight. This of course repeated the manœuvres of the previous night which seemed to have proved effective in misleading the enemy. In subsequent analysis of German records, it is clear that the alteration had not been noticed and that it must have upset the plans of the attacking U-boats.

The course of the convoy during most of the night would be about easterly. The wind was blowing moderately strongly from between south and south-west, so it was thought that the majority of U-boat attacks would come from the starboard side, and if the northern lights appeared again, which fortunately did not happen, then the chances of attacks from starboard were increased, with the ships silhouetted against the lights.

However, as the alteration to port might force an attack from that side early in the night, the escorts were disposed equally on both sides of the convoy. Fortunately all radar and asdic sets were still in action.

The *Alisma* was stationed on the starboard bow, the *Pink* on the starboard beam and the *Tay* on the starboard quarter. On the port side, the *Loosestrife* was on the bow, the *Vidette* on the beam and the *Snowflake* on the quarter with a watching brief over the rear ships of the convoy. Station-keeping was good and the convoy was becoming a well-drilled body of ships.

A policy for the night was issued to the escorts in which the escort commander said that he hoped to get warning of most submarine attacks from the H/F D/F office. He also reminded escorts that they must fire a starshell at once at radar contacts, and he stressed that there would not be time for prolonged hunts of U-boats. Escorts must carry out a quick counter-attack and once satisfied that the U-boat was no longer a danger to the convoy must return to their station to be ready to repel the next attempt.

By 2000, the convoy had almost completed its turn to port and was steering 070°. It was not long before excitement began. First came H/F D/F indications of submarines on both bows with the strongest signals coming from starboard; the group was warned accordingly on convoy wave.

Then occurred one of the most extraordinary incidents of the whole battle. Kplt Mumm of *U594* reports having surfaced by mistake in the middle of the convoy at 2012. He could see at least six merchant ships and one escort. But apparently he considered that he was too close to the ships to fire torpedoes so he steamed at full speed on convoy course, still on the surface, in order to get ahead into a position for firing.

The fact that Mumm could see an escort, and his subsequent operations, show that he must have surfaced between the twelfth and thirteenth columns.

This illustrates vividly the difficulties of sighting a submarine with its low silhouette on a dark night. The high speed must have raised a bow wave and a wake astern, but no look-outs can have sighted the boat for no reports were made.

It is interesting to reflect on the reactions of the German 'aces' to the conduct of the *U594*. They were accustomed to remaining in the middle of the convoy, coolly picking off their target one by one, and they would have expected the *U594* to do the same. But fortunately for the convoy Mumm must have decided that he needed more sea room.

Soon after the submarine had emerged from the columns of the convoy, an alert radar operator in the *Alisma* noticed at 2025 a small echo which seemed to be ahead of the leading ship of the starboard-wing column.

The captain of the *Alisma* naturally assumed that this was a U-boat trying to penetrate the screen, so he turned towards the target and prepared for an immediate counter-attack, reporting accordingly to the escort commander. But the plotting-table soon estimated, surprisingly but correctly, that the submarine was steering the same course as the convoy. Radar contact was lost at 1,000 yards as the U-boat dived, and asdic contact was gained at a range of 450 yards soon afterwards.

The contact was well out to starboard, as I imagine that the captain expected the U-boat to turn towards the convoy. It was not possible to carry out an accurate attack, and ten depth-charges set to shallow were dropped, more as a scaring effort than one likely to cause damage.

Lieutenant-Commander Rose then reckoned that he must get back to his station on the bow, but immediately, to his surprise, the radar operator reported at 2056 yet another contact, also ahead of the convoy. The range was 2,000 yards and a star-shell was immediately fired over the target. Two minutes later the sinister shape of a conning-tower was sighted.

Shortly afterwards, the submarine dived, but no asdic contact was gained. Again a 'scaring' attack was made and ten depth-charges set to shallow were dropped in the estimated position of the U-boat, at 2106.

In his report, Rose expresses uncertainty as to whether one or two U-boats were involved in the incident, but analysis shows that it is most likely to have been two. Whether one or two boats were there, however, no attack was made on the convoy which must have watched with some alarm the firing of a star-shell and the dropping of depth-charges ahead of the starboard wing.

The Admiralty U-boat Assessment Committee estimated that

there was 'insufficient evidence of damage' and the *U594* records that the depth-charges exploded 'at a distance'.

The *Alisma*, as she took up her position on the bow again, must have felt well pleased that one and possibly two attacks had been thwarted. It is more difficult to imagine the feelings of the captain of *U594*. He cannot have been satisfied with his performance in not firing a single torpedo, but on the other hand, the sudden attack on a dark night must have been a very alarming experience, and he may have believed himself lucky to escape. The *U594* took no further active part in the operations against convoy HX231.

There was little time to relax before the next attack. At 2120, a signal was received from the *Loosestrife* on the port bow that she had fired a star-shell at a suspected contact ahead, a signal which cleared up an already uncertain situation. The circumstances of the incident make unhappy reading: almost every mistake possible was made. But the bad must be recorded as well as the good, and it has already been indicated that after a change in command, the *Loosestrife* quickly became an efficient ship.

To begin with, no signalled report was made of the first radar contact which was at 2105, and the first the escort commander knew was the sight of star-shell bursting in the sky. Any illumination could indicate that a ship had been torpedoed, so he sent off a general signal, 'Interrogate Ignite', which asked what the illumination was about, and he had some worrying moments before the explanatory signal was received at 2120.

Meanwhile the *Loosestrife* had been steering for the contact which appeared to be ahead of the leading ships of the second or third columns. But during the noise of the star-shell firing, a bad mistake was made on the *Loosestrife*'s quarter-deck, and two depth-charges were released in error. They were set to shallow, the ship had not yet reached her correct speed, and as a result of the shock of the explosion, both the asdic and the radar sets became temporarily defective.

Soon afterwards, a conning-tower was sighted just ahead of one of the merchant ships and she altered course to try to ram. But she lost sight of the submarine at a range of about 1,000 yards and it must have dived. Then the *Loosestrife* found herself manœuvring inside the convoy and having difficulty in avoiding collision with the merchant ships. Fortunately by now the radar and asdic sets were working again.

It must have been an alarming and confusing situation, but I believe that it should have been possible to drop a depth-charge pattern near the diving position of the submarine, set to deep so that it could not harm the merchant ships. This would have been an additional precaution against the U-boat's firing any torpedoes. It should also have been possible to fire the foremost gun at the submarine while it was still ahead of the convoy, but the captain of the *Loosestrife* feared that one of the merchant ships might have been hit in error. Altogether ten star-shells were fired and the U-boat was fully illuminated.

The corvette then returned to her position on the port bow, and despite a chapter of accidents and mistakes, the U-boat had at least been forced to dive before making any attack.

It is difficult to determine which U-boat was involved in this incident, which does not appear in any log book. Perhaps it was one of the submarines which were lost in other operations before returning to harbour, so that the log book will never be found. The captain must have had a frightening experience and he was lucky not to have been rammed by one of the merchant ships, for his position was well lit-up by the light of the star-shell.

The *Loosestrife* was back in station by 2148, but before then, at 2125, the H/F D/F office was giving warning of strong signals close on the port beam. The *Vidette* was immediately dispatched to search on the bearing, but found nothing. There can be little doubt, however, that a submarine must have been present and that it was driven off by the quick sweep out of the *Vidette*, which was back in station by 2225.

At this stage, the escort commander, under the influence of a rather optimistic appreciation of the situation by the H/F D/F office, made a code message to the group on convoy wave which read: 'There seems to be one still ahead; the rest of the team has retired to the rear with headaches.' Unfortunately, although there was certainly considerable radio activity astern, there was still more than one submarine ahead as will soon be seen.

The *Pink* was at action stations with the engine-room ready for full speed at short notice. At 2137, the radar operator reported a firm contact to the eastward at a range of 2,400 yards – which was on the starboard bow of the convoy. The ship turned towards the contact, which was plotted and found to be moving fast towards the convoy.

This, we now know, was the *U270* which had noticed the gap between the *Alisma* and the *Pink* in the light of the star-shell from the *Loosestrife* and had made for the convoy at best speed. Oblt Otto reports firing two torpedoes and claims to have hit two tankers, one of 4,000 and one of 6,000 tons. But his claim was false and no ships were hit; perhaps he confused the explosion of the *Pink*'s depth-charges with the noise of torpedo-hits.

For the *Pink*, which had fired a star-shell without sighting the U-boat, lost radar contact at 600 yards, having previously picked up the U-boat on asdic, and had thus forced it to dive by a smart counter-attack. The *Pink* held asdic contact until only 100 yards away, and was able to carry out a good depth-charge attack at 2142 with the ten charges set to shallow. At no time was the U-boat sighted, but the phosphorescence of its wake was clearly seen.

The *U270* reported that only a few electric fuses had blown in the attack. The Admiralty U-boat Assessment Committee, having considered all the evidence, which included a statement that a blue flash was seen by men on the *Pink*'s deck, came to the conclusion that the attack had been a useful one but that there was not enough evidence to assess the damage.

After making the first attack, the *Pink* opened the range and turned preparatory to having another try, but the asdic contact which was immediately reported was considered to come from the water disturbed by the explosion of the first depth-charge pattern. After a short search, the *Pink* was ordered to return to her station.

The captain of the *U270* was a determined man. He remained submerged for less than two hours and then set off at best speed to get into position ahead of the convoy for an attack just after dawn. His task was made easier by the constant illumination caused by the attempted attacks of his colleagues during the night which pinpointed the position of the convoy and of the escorts for his benefit.

There was not much time to wait before the next incident, with the ever alert *Alisma* again engaged. At 2150, eight minutes after the *Pink*'s *U270* had dived, the *Alisma* which had only just regained her station on the bow got yet another radar contact of a U-boat to the southward which appeared to be trying to penetrate the screen between the ship and the *Pink*. Again the *Alisma* turned towards the target and again star-shells were fired. The U-boat then seemed to have turned away from the convoy and dived, for at 2158 radar contact was lost. A full pattern of depth-charges was dropped in the estimated position, using both stop-watch and plot to determine the time for firing. The attack was claimed as being no more than 'harassing', but it succeeded in preventing an attack on the convoy.

In his remarks on this attack, the commodore at Derry said that it was possible that both the *Alisma* and the *Pink* may have attacked the same submarine. But after a careful search of the German records, it appears that he was wrong, and that two submarines were present.

Immediately after dropping depth-charges, the *Alisma* resumed station on the screen, informing the escort commander accordingly.

There was then a comparative lull for an hour when at 2315, some more star-shells were seen on the starboard bow and the escort commander asked over convoy wave what was happening. There is no sign in the records of any attack by an escort, but from the signal log it is evident that the *Pink* must have got another radar contact and illuminated it with a star-shell. No submarine success followed, so the *Pink* must have driven off the U-boat.

Shortly after this, at 2330, the convoy started to alter course back to starboard to 100°. This process, it will be remembered, took a long time, and was completed by about midnight.

At 2355, the H/F D/F office obtained a strong signal on the starboard bow and all escorts were warned to be alert. At 0035, the *Alisma* reported sighting a flash in the convoy and the escort commander asked the commodore if he had anything to report.

He received the reply 'negative'. It had been feared, of course, that a ship had been torpedoed, but fortunately nothing had occurred and it will never be known what caused the flash.

It is difficult to describe adequately the tension during the night. Complete darkness, when it was difficult to see adjacent ships, alternated with the bright glow of star-shells which made everyone feel 'naked' to attack. The weather was poor and the look-outs had to contend with strong wind and sometimes spray. On the bridges it was easy to make mistakes, and coolness of decision had to be matched with speed.

It was not long before the latest warning from the H/F D/F office bore fruit, and now it was to be the frigate *Tay* on the starboard quarter of the convoy which was to take the brunt of the battle.

This time no radar contact was obtained. As the ship was altering course on the starboard leg of the zigzag, a U-boat was suddenly sighted steaming across the *Tay*'s bows at a range of only about 150 yards and obviously bound for the convoy. At the same time, the asdic operator reported 'hydrophone effect' ahead.

Everything happened very quickly. The rudder was reversed, the engines put to full ahead, the guns were ordered to open fire and a small searchlight was switched on to the U-boat.

But the submarine got across the *Tay*'s bows and by then was within her turning circle so that ramming was impossible. The guns were blazing and the tracer of the Oerlikon could be easily followed. The first few rounds were over the target and then hits obtained, and it is not known whether the only round of 4-in. which was fired hit or not. The crew claimed a hit on the conning-tower.

Then, when the U-boat was about 800 yards away, it dived and fortunately the asdic set immediately gained contact. What seemed to be a good attack was then carried out with fourteen depth-charges set to explode at shallow.

The ship ran out to about 1,000 yards, turned and picked up an asdic contact which seemed to be stopped very close to the original explosion. Immediately, another attack with fourteen charges was made, and after the explosion the asdic operator reported that he could hear the U-boat blowing tanks, which would be done in order to come to the surface. A heavy explosion followed, rising to the surface in a dull red glow which was seen by the look-outs.

After the second attack, the *Tay*'s steering-gear broke down temporarily and using the main engines to keep on course, she returned to the convoy.

The captain's assessment was that both attacks had been accurate and that the U-boat had probably been sunk.

In the report of the Admiralty Committtee, it is noted that two submarines were known to have been sunk during the passage of the convoy, one by an aircraft. The *Tay* was therefore awarded a 'probably sunk' for her attacks. Subsequent records show that *U635* made no signals after 5 April and it was therefore assumed that this was the submarine sunk by the *Tay*.

So far, so good. But unfortunately, a very careful analysis of the times of the attack and a comparison between the reports by the U-boats and those by the *Tay*, show that owing to the full picture not being available during the war, a mistake assessment of claim may well have been made.

Firstly, the Assessment Committee's report shows that the *Tay*'s attack took place at 0451, whereas there is no doubt that it took place at 0051 on 6 April. Secondly, the *U306* reports that at 0030 it was caught in a searchlight beam but remained on the surface. An escort came suddenly rushing down on the U-boat, firing red and green tracer. At first, the salvoes were too high, and the U-boat remained on the surface and tried to get away. When hits were obtained on the conning-tower and on the upper deck, the U-boat dived deep. A depth-charge pursuit then started.

The two times do not correspond exactly, but I find that German timing of U-boat incidents is often approximate, and in this case may have referred to the time of sighting the convoy, which would explain the small discrepancy. In any case, the similarity between the two accounts must be more than a coincidence and furthermore, no other escort fired on an identified submarine within three hours of the *Tay*'s attack. I have checked and cross-checked the *Tay*'s timing from several different sources and am convinced that it is correct.

Reluctantly one must conclude, therefore, that the *Tay*'s U-boat was the *U306* which reported no damage from the encounter. The submarine remained submerged for over two hours, and then finding itself well astern of the convoy, broke off the operation and steered for the 'Milch Cow' tanker to refuel.

It had been a very exciting affair for the frigate and all were pleased to get their first sight of a German submarine at night at such close quarters. It had been a shock for all concerned, especially as no radar warning had been received. The depth-charge crews had worked well and reloading of the second pattern had been quickly carried out in the dark: not an easy matter, especially when the ship was rolling and pitching. In the light of subsequent analysis, it seems that the second pattern was dropped on the disturbance in the water left by the first attack, and this probability is confirmed by the track chart from the plotting-table.

The gunnery had not been so effective, though hits were eventually obtained. Paradoxically, the range was too short and the change of bearing of the target too quick. The guns had been exercised at night at a far greater range, and one of the first actions of the escort commander on return to harbour was to devise a new exercise called 'Pointblank' which practised firing at very short range.

I have allowed much space to the *Tay*'s battle with the *U306*, for it illustrates so many interesting points, such as the drama of close-range action at night, the toughness of the U-boats (for the first pattern must have exploded close to the submarine), and the difficulties facing the Admiralty Assessment Committee.

The *Tay* did not take long to regain station and there is a record of a signal to the *Snowflake* on convoy wave at 0118, warning her that the frigate was catching up from astern, so as to avoid mistakes in identification.

To make the narrative more difficult to set out, convoy time changed at 0200 and clocks were advanced to 0300 (+1). The next incident, at 0310 new time, took place only one hour therefore after the last one.

H/F D/F activity had continued with all signals coming from astern where, it was assumed, the submarines were reporting their lack of success. The next attack, at 0310, came without any warning from the H/F D/F set, and again it was the alert *Alisma* which provided the defence. The weather was deteriorating, the wind and sea increasing and the radar contact of the submarine was picked up at only 2,000 yards. The U-boat seemed to be trying to penetrate the screen between the *Alisma* and the *Pink* so an immediate counter-attack was started. Star-shells were fired and the submarine sighted, so the Oerlikon guns opened fire. Radar contact was lost at 1,000 yards, when the U-boat dived, but fortunately the asdic picked it up almost at once. It was moving 'rapidly right' towards the convoy, so the ship altered 30° to starboard and was able to hold asdic contact down to 100 yards. The chemical recorder was working well and the attack was delivered with seven depth-charges set to shallow. Three charges had failed to roll out of the trap in the stern for some reason which was never established. A flare was dropped to mark the spot and the *Alisma* swept back twice near the original position without getting any contact.

The captain's estimate was that the attack had been a good one and the submarine was probably damaged. The Admiralty Committee was less optimistic and assessed 'insufficient evidence of damage', but this attack must be remembered for later reference for I can find no report from any U-boat of the incident and it may well be that *U635* was sunk.

The next event of this long and busy night was presaged by a strong radio signal from the ground-wave on the starboard bow, which was heard in the H/F D/F office at 0345. Warning was passed to all escorts on convoy wave and the *Vidette* was instructed to move from the port beam to a position ahead of the centre of the convoy to reinforce the defence in the forward sector. Only two attacks had been attempted from the port side, there were no more signals in that direction and the *Vidette* seemed to be insufficiently employed.

At this time the *Snowflake* was engaged in one of those irritating domestic scenes of convoy life which so diverted attention from the enemy. The *Jamaica Planter*, the ship of the vice-commodore, had developed steering-gear trouble and had had to drop astern.

As a result, the *Snowflake* spent a worrying half-hour screening this large ship with a valuable cargo until the damage had been repaired and then led her back to her station.

But we must return to the starboard side of the convoy and to the *Pink* which was in station on the beam. At 0415, alerted no doubt by the warning from the H/F D/F bearings, the *Pink* obtained a firm radar contact ahead of the ship at a range of 4,800 yards. This was the greatest detection range of the night and showed much efficiency in the way the set was operated and maintained.

The U-boat was moving fast towards the convoy and the *Pink*, which had increased speed, delayed firing a star-shell in the hope of surprising the submarine and ramming it.

The ship's course was constantly adjusted to keep the submarine on the starboard bow, the range was reduced very rapidly and at 1,200 yards, a star-shell was fired from the 4-in. gun. At a range of 800 yards, the U-boat was sighted, not even trimmed down, and showing a high bow wave. Fire was opened with the 4-in. and Oerlikon guns and hits were seen from the latter on the conning-tower. The star-shell illumination was remarkably good, and it was not until after the action that Lieutenant Atkinson realized that the *Alisma* had helped him by keeping a star-shell in the air while his 4-in. gun was otherwise occupied firing high explosive!

The U-boat then started to carry out some sharp evasive turns on the surface which were difficult to follow. After a small turn towards the convoy, it suddenly turned quickly away to starboard and crashed-dived. This last turn was not seen immediately. The *Pink* altered course towards the diving position and soon picked up a good asdic contact, but the turn had been too late, and the submarine passed down the starboard side at a range of 250 yards. The order to fire a depth-charge pattern was countermanded as the range was too great and the *Pink* opened out again to try to regain asdic contact. But there was no success and after two sweeps through the probable positions, she went back to her place on the screen.

In his report, Lieutenant Atkinson says that he should probably have fired his depth-charge pattern, but that he did not do so because he knew that it could not damage the U-boat; because he had already expended over one-third of his stock of depth-charges; and because he hoped to open the range, pick up contact and attack again.

There is no doubt that the submarine concerned was the *U706*, commanded by the determined von Zitzewitz, who had sunk the *British Ardour*. He reports having been illuminated at 0412 by the escorts' star-shell when just about to attack the convoy. He said that he was spotted and had to crash-dive deep. He also reported that the escort passed overhead but did not drop depth-charges. He remained submerged for three hours and made no more attempts on the convoy during the night.

The *Alisma* had played a useful part in this affair and had kept the illumination going when it was most needed. It must not have been easy to follow both the movements of the submarine and the other escort, and at one time the captain found it necessary to take urgent avoiding action to miss the *Pink*. Several officers reported seeing a torpedo pass close astern of the *Alisma* during the action though the captain did not sight it himself.

The night's activities were not over yet, though they were now to decrease. At 0425, the group was warned that there were probably two more submarines on the starboard bow. There had been more signalling, bearings of which had been taken in the H/F D/F office where the officer and the operator were tired but still very alert.

The *U134* reported in the log that a steamer had been sighted on the starboard side of the convoy at 0450, and that it was preparing to attack. Nothing developed, however, and one can only con-clude that the submarine was deterred by the presence of three escorts on that side, the *Alisma*, the *Pink* and the *Tay*. It is irritating to find the *U134* stating that it prepared to fire a 'fan' shot of three torpedoes, but giving no reason for the failure to fire.

This was the final attempt of the night, and the escorts had succeeded in beating off every attack. There was no question of relaxing, for they did not know how many submarines were still ahead. However, the radio traffic stopped and the H/F D/F log shows a gap of some hours.

In his signalled reports to the Commander-in-Chief Western Approaches, the escort commander claimed to have driven off no less than sixteen attempts to attack the convoy during the night. This may have been so, though the official records show some ten or eleven. At this distance of time, it is not possible to judge whether the signals contained an element of euphoric exaggeration, or whether some of the submarine attempts to attack were not documented.

Then at about 0500, tragedy struck. The weather had been getting steadily worse all through the night and the gallant *Waroonga* which had been keeping perfect station, found that her main bulkheads were starting to buckle. It was clear that the ship could not continue to steam, so the engines were stopped, the *Loosestrife* was warned of the situation and the master gave the order to abandon ship. The story of the rescue of the survivors of this brave ship is recounted later.

Some redeployment of the escort was now needed. The *Vidette* which was stationed ahead of the convoy was ordered to screen the *Loosestrife* and an American ship, the *J. R. Poinsett*, which had also stopped to help with survivors. It was an unjustified risk to leave three ships stopped astern of the convoy, so the *Vidette* circled them in order to discourage any attack by U-boats.

This left the screen unbalanced; and the *Snowflake* was brought up on the port bow, and the *Tay* was told to replace the *Vidette* ahead of the centre columns of the convoy. There was just time for this move to be completed before dawn, when submerged attack from periscope depth might be expected by any U-boat still ahead of the convoy.

The loss, for she sank soon after being abandoned, of the *Waroonga* was a sad blow after what had proved to be a most successful night.

At least ten, and probably more attacks had been driven off, three U-boats had been engaged with gunfire and several more with depth-charges. All the escorts of the convoy had been busy in one way or another and the results had exceeded the wildest expectations. When dawn broke and still no ship had been hit, the escort commander was a proud man.

Thought should be spared for the officers and men of the merchant ships. The light of star-shell flares, the bark of gunfire and the explosions of depth-charges had continued for almost the whole night. They must have felt very 'naked' in the glare of the star-shells; everyone knew that a torpedo might hit them at any moment, and nerves were taut.

The commodore of the convoy wrote in his report that he considered that the operations of the night 'had been a brilliant piece of work by a small escort group when conditions were favourable for attack'. This is a welcome tribute to discover some thirty years after the event.

There remains the difficult problem of how the *U635* was sunk, and the probability is that it was lost during the attacks of the night of 5/6 April which have just been described.

The timing and the remarkable similarity between the reports of the *Tay* and the *U306* lead to the firm conclusion that the *Tay* cannot have been responsible for the *U635*. Who was responsible? The records of both sides have been studied and it is not possible to come to any firm conclusion.

There is no German report of the attack by the *Alisma* at 0315 on 6 April: an attack which was considered accurate. So this may have been the *U635*. The other attack by the *Alisma* which is not accompanied by a corresponding German report for the same time was most unlikely to have been responsible. The attack was inaccurate and delivered more to scare the enemy than to damage him, as asdic contact was lost very early on in the attack.

It is possible that the *U635* was rammed by a merchant ship, and unlike his colleague in the *U572*, was sunk and not damaged. But this seems extremely unlikely. The shock of a collision which actually sank a submarine was bound to be severe and must have been reported.

No one will ever know the correct answer, but probably the credit should go to the *Alisma* for her attack at 0315. It would certainly be a well-earned reward for a great night's work.

# 8

# The Day of 6 April and Night of 6/7

The first incident of the day of Tuesday, 6 April was mysterious. The *U134*, commanded by Oblt Brosin and which had been driven off by convoy escorts only two hours earlier, claims to have fired three torpedoes at 0600(+1) at a 4,000-ton straggler, all of which missed. So far as the records show, only one ship was then well astern of the convoy, the *J. R. Poinsett*, which had picked up forty-one survivors of the *Waroonga* and was being escorted back to station by the *Loosestrife*. No torpedoes were sighted and no damage was done. Nor apparently did any one hear the torpedoes exploding at the end of their run as sometimes happened.

The only possible clue to the mystery is that the *Snowflake*, which was stationed on the port side of the convoy reported having seen a flare at 0520, which is forty minutes before the *U134* logged as the time when three torpedoes were fired which missed. The discrepancy in time is large, however, and it is difficult to link the two incidents.

Whatever happened, it was fortunate that the *J. R. Poinsett* with her additional passengers was not hit, thus subjecting the *Waroonga* survivors to yet another dreadful ordeal.

After making this abortive attack, the *U134*, which had little fuel remaining, broke off the operation and returned to its home port in the Bay of Biscay.

The situation around the convoy was temporarily quiet and there was no radio activity heard by the H/F D/F office. The weather had continued to get worse, wind and sea were strong from the south-west, visibility had dropped to less than two miles, and the cloud base was low. It was a horrible day.

But prospects generally seemed brighter as both the support group and the escorting aircraft were due shortly. Moreover, the escort commander did not believe that the submarines could remain in contact in such conditions, though he was wrong, for by diving and listening on hydrophones, several U-boats remained in firm contact throughout the day, despite the fact that they never got a glimpse of the convoy.

The escort commander would also have been disappointed to learn that sixteen boats were still operating against the convoy, as is plain from the entries in the German War Diary for 6 April!

Control sent another long signal to Group *Löwenherz* during the forenoon. It said that in spite of tolerable weather conditions, results so far had been disappointing. It accused too many boats of chasing after stragglers and pointed out that it was the convoy which was the main target and that U-boats must concentrate on it. If there should be air cover with the convoy today, and if in spite of it, contact was maintained, U-boats should get around ahead of the convoy at maximum speed, keeping thirty to forty miles away, with the object of attacking from ahead. Every opportunity must be taken to get to grips with the convoy much more energetically and with greater tenacity.

This signal reflects all the faults of armchair experts on submarine warfare. First, it was natural to attack stragglers which were defenceless without an escort, though in the case of the *Sunoil* and the *Blitar*, as we shall see later, too many U-boats left the convoy to chase these two ships.

But in view of the way in which attacks had been pressed home during the night of 5/6, the accusation of lack of urgency seems unfair. It strikes the neutral observer that the U-boat headquarters had not appreciated the effect of the combination of the new short-wave radar and of the H/F D/F set when used by a trained group. In fact, the signal failed in its object of producing more massed attacks on the convoy.

As will be remembered, there were four destroyers, detached from the Home Fleet at Scapa Flow, which were expected to join shortly in the support role. There was the *Inglefield*, whose captain, Commander A. G. West, was senior officer of the group; the *Eclipse* (Lieutenant-Commander E. Mack); the *Fury* (Lieutenant-Commander C. W. Campbell); and the *Icarus* (Lieutenant-Commander E. N. Walmsley). They were fleet-type destroyers, built in the thirties, which had formed the backbone of the destroyer force at the start of the war.

The *Inglefield* and the *Icarus* were fitted with H/F D/F sets which was a great advantage.

It would be easier to listen out on the various radio frequencies which the U-boats were using and it might be possible to fix accurately the position of a transmitting U-boat by getting bearings from more than one ship.

These destroyers were more familiar with escorting battleships and aircraft carriers with the Home Fleet and were not very experienced with Atlantic trade convoys. They would be very welcome, however. There was one slight worry in the escort commander's mind. It was the first time he had had a support group in company, and the policy was that the senior officer of the close escort should direct the activities of the support group. It was perfectly logical. He knew the convoy, he knew his own escorts, he was up to date with the U-boat situation and he was responsible for controlling the aircraft which escorted the convoy. But it was not a pleasant thought to have to give orders to an officer who was considerably more senior. However, by making polite requests about the stationing and movements of the support-group ships, all went well and the two groups worked together in harmony.

In addition, a flying programme had been arranged – details of which had been received during the night – which was intended to provide constant air escort in daylight. The first Liberator from Iceland was expected soon after dawn, and the Germans were not going to have an easy time if the weather allowed the programme to be fulfilled.

The second incident of the day was an exciting one. The *Tay* was changing from full action stations to defence stations, when half the ship's company would be on watch, and the ship was zigzagging about 2,000 yards ahead of the commodore's column which was in the centre of the convoy. The sea was fairly rough, the wind strong from the south-west and the visibility still poor. The convoy was steering east.

At 0647, when the *Tay* was just altering course on to the star-

94

board leg of her zigzag, an asdic contact was reported at a range of 900 yards, bearing 045°, which was on her port bow.

After a long and tiring night, the report was not at first treated as seriously as it deserved, but the ship was turned towards the target and the operator then firmly classified the echo as 'submarine'. He stuck to his assertion, and he was absolutely right, for when the range was about 100 yards, the stern of a submarine could be seen sticking out of the water, and it was obvious that it was moving fast towards the convoy, i.e. to the left. The colour of the hull of the boat was a browny grey, and presented a memorable sight. In fact some officers were so astonished that they could not believe their eyes, and the bridge rang with picturesque language as they were informed fully of the situation!

It was none other than our old enemy, the *U270*, the captain of which must have brought the boat to periscope depth for a last look before firing torpedoes at the convoy. He must then have sighted the *Tay* bearing down on him and ordered a crash-dive. Oblt Otto was a cool commanding officer as, in his report, he does not mention the crash-dive but merely notes that he was detected by asdic, that he was depth-charged and that his attack was abortive!

The angle of the crash-dive was too great, however, and for this, the engineer officer, who in German submarines was responsible for diving and surfacing procedures, must take the blame for having allowed the submarine's stern to stick up out of the water.

It was too late for the *Tay* to ram: the boat was too close and inside her turning circle, and at the last moment, just before the depth-charge pattern was released, the wheel was put to starboard, thus kicking the stern to port and getting the depth-charges a little closer to the U-boat.

Owing to a serious mistake, due probably to the firing taking place during a changeover of crews, only five depth-charges were dropped instead of the ten ordered. The charge from the port thrower was seen to fall very close to the submarine, which promptly disappeared below the surface. All charges had been set to shallow, which was fifty feet. The time was 0650, only three minutes after the first contact.

There was little opportunity to ruminate on the results of the attack, for by now the columns of the convoy were fast bearing down on the scene and the main problem was to avoid collision with the commodore's ship. But Lieutenant-Commander Sherwood was very determined and a fine ship-handler. He succeeded in turning his ship between the seventh and eighth columns – the captain of the *Port Sydney* afterwards complained good-humouredly that he had had to go astern to avoid colliding with the *Tay* – and at 0802 a full fourteen-charge pattern was released near the position of the original attack with a depth setting of 300 feet. But no further asdic contact had been made – it was always difficult inside a convoy – and the attack was more for discouragement than anything else. It succeeded, for *U270* fired no torpedoes and did not surface until three hours later, when it was well clear of the convoy. It reports having been harried by destroyers and aircraft throughout the afternoon, and in the evening, it broke off the operation altogether.

A brave attack had been thwarted by an alert asdic operator.

Meanwhile the *Tay* had continued to chase the *U270* and had twice to pass through the columns to do so. It was a hair-raising effort in the low visibility and well carried out, but without any contact being gained.

There was a final dramatic scene to this remarkable affair. When the second pattern of depth-charges had been released, in accordance with custom a flare had been thrown over the side to mark the spot. For some unknown reason which was probably connected with the strain of the night before, several merchant ships in the convoy mistook the canister of the flare for a periscope! Gunfire of every description was directed at the flare and the size of the shells seemed to vary between 4-in. and machine-guns. The *Tay* was lucky to escape damage and it seemed a miracle that no ship in the convoy was apparently hit. A quick signal was made to the commodore, who ordered 'cease firing' by radio and the panic subsided.

I suspect that the guns crews had been closed-up at their stations all night, that they were tired and jittery, and the opportunity to 'have a go' was too good to miss. It was an alarming incident.

Meanwhile, the escort commander had ordered the *Pink* to join in the search for the U-boat responsible, but without success; and soon the *Tay* had moved off to resume her station ahead of the convoy, as the escort was thin with the *Loosestrife* and the *Vidette* still astern with survivors of the *Waroonga*.

The *Tay* captain's report assessed the result of the attack as having severely shaken the enemy; the Admiralty Assessment Committee said 'insufficient evidence of damage' and this is confirmed by the War Diary of the *U270*.

Nevertheless, credit must be given to the *Tay* for a smart counter-attack which undoubtedly prevented the *U270* from sinking some ships in the convoy. The asdic operator who insisted so firmly that his contact was that of a submarine also deserves special praise and the recognition which he subsequently received.

It is interesting to reflect on the difference between the attack by *U706* on the *British Ardour* when the submarine passed close to both the *Tay* and the *Loosestrife* without detection, whereas the *U270* was quickly picked up. There could not be a clearer example of the difference between good and bad water conditions in asdic operations, nor of the difficulty of providing an impregnable defence for ships against U-boat attack.

As to the remainder of the pack, we know from the German records that the *U260* regained contact at about this time and signalled the position of the convoy, but the signal was not received in the *Tay*'s H/F D/F office and must have been transmitted on a frequency on which watch was not being kept.

Shortly after the *Tay*'s second depth-charge attack, the escort commander and his staff were severely tested, for not only did the first Liberator aircraft of the day join, but three ships of the support group also arrived.

At about 0800, Liberator E of 120 Squadron from Iceland reached the convoy. It was homed successfully and had taken off some four hours previously under the command of Flying Officer Moffatt. Owing to the dearth of H/F D/F bearings of U-boats, the escort commander could give no positive indication of the position of the submarines, so he asked the pilot to fly around the convoy at a distance of about ten miles, keeping a special watch on the stern position where some U-boats must still be. He also gave him full information about the support group.

Conditions for flying were appalling. There was ten-tenths cloud and the cloud base was only 700 feet. In the prevailing visibility, visual signalling was impossible and convoy-wave radio telephone was used to pass the messages. All went smoothly, however, and the Liberator proceeded on her mission. Under these conditions, the white-painted aircraft with their radar should be able to catch the submarines by surprise.

The support group also had to be given an outline of the position generally and requested to take up its positions. The senior officer had some information to pass too, notably that the *Fury* had lost her asdic dome in bad weather and would be no good in asdic operations.

Signalling by light was a nightmare, for in addition to the bad weather and poor visibility, the *Tay* was weaving her way back through the convoy to her station ahead, so that ships would keep obstructing the signals at vital moments. After much expenditure of effort, and after sending one long signal to the wrong ship all the necessary messages had been passed.

The *Inglefield* and the *Eclipse* were asked to take over the hunt for the *Tay*'s submarine from the *Pink*, for only the *Snowflake* and the *Alisma* were in their screening stations, and the defence was weak.

The *Fury* was put in the stern position on the close screen, where her lack of asdics was less important and where she could use her radar to deal with U-boats on the surface and with stragglers.

The *Icarus* joined an hour later, and started to move off towards the extended screen ahead of the convoy, but her asdics, too, broke down, and she was recalled to the close screen.

The *Inglefield* and the *Eclipse* failed to find the *Tay*'s submarine, though the captain of U270 complained bitterly that he had been harried unmercifully. So after an hour's hunt, they were recalled and, as the only two fully effective ships of the support group, were put on the extended screen about five miles from the convoy The *Inglefield* with H/F D/F was put on the starboard bow, so as to give the maximum base line for fixing enemy submarines in conjunction with the *Tay*, and the *Eclipse* was on the port bow.

As well as all this signal activity with the aircraft and the support group, a long report had to be sent of the night's proceedings to the commander-in-chief ashore who needed to be kept up to date with events. Only a very efficient staff officer and communication team could have competed with this involved task, especially as the escort commander, who had had little rest during the past three days, chose that moment to lose his voice, and his handwriting was not very clear!

The load was now on the aircraft and the ships of the support group, especially the former, which carried out their role magnificently. Unfortunately, not one single bearing was received in the H/F D/F offices from dawn until just after the last Liberator left at 1935, a little before darkness fell. So the ships were unable to help by directing the aircraft on to submarines.

In his report, the escort commander assumed that no signals had been sent because of the very strong air cover, but signals were in fact picked up by radio stations ashore, and the Admiralty was able to confirm that the convoy was still being shadowed. It will always be a mystery why these signals were not heard by the ships.

Within two hours of dawn, three Liberators were escorting the convoy. At 0901, T of 120 Squadron arrived after no less than eight hours' flying. Homing procedure had not been as successful as it should have been, and the aircraft arrived later than Liberator E of the same squadron, although it had taken off some time earlier

Then X of 120 Squadron arrived after a perfect homing drill, having spent only three and a half hours in transit. Good communication on convoy wave R/T was established with all three aircraft and it was now possible to saturate the area within twenty or thirty miles of the convoy with air cover. The results were impressive.

At 1045, the *Vidette* was back with the convoy, having brought up the *Loosestrife* and the *J. R. Poinsett* with survivors of the

*Waroonga* and the close screen was beginning to get back to full strength again. In fact, there were now six ships of B7 Group with all facilities fully effective and the two destroyers without asdic.

The *Vidette* reported that there were three stragglers from the convoy: visibility was now down to only one mile and one had to rely on radar to keep an eye on the ships. Difficulties of station-keeping in convoy were great and it is to the credit of the merchant ships that the formation was so good. It seemed that the stragglers were in the greatest danger from U-boats, so the *Eclipse* was asked to escort them back to the convoy. No. 134, the *Aruba* and No. 75, the *Mossdale* were back in station by the afternoon, but No. 41, the *Laurelwood* took much longer to get back and did not rejoin until dawn next day, 7 April.

From now on, attacks by aircraft on U-boats form the main part of the narrative of the day's proceedings, so it might be helpful to the reader to be given a brief description of what happened in a typical U-boat which made a crash-drive after sighting an aircraft.

'Aircraft on the port bow' reported one of the German look-outs, and 'clear the bridge' shouted the officer of the watch who also pressed the alarm bells which ordered an emergency dive. The target time for clearing the bridge was five seconds only, and this needed much practice, especially when the men were encumbered by heavy-weather oilskins and thick clothing. Men down below stood by to catch them as they scrambled through the narrow hatch down the ladder into the hull. In this particular case, the officer of the watch who was always the last to go down, took rather more than five seconds before he shut the hatch, turned the locking handwheel and shouted 'flood'. The water then started to pour into the diving-tanks to give additional weight to the boat and force it down.

Meanwhile, there was great activity. The diesel engines were stopped; and the electric motors were coupled up and took over the propulsion of the boat. Various air intakes and exhaust valves were closed and a host of other jobs carried out. It was vital for each man to carry out his part of the drill perfectly, not only so as to dive quickly, but to dive safely.

At the order 'flood', the foremost diving-tanks had been filled first and the after tanks last in order that the bows would go down; the boat was gradually getting heavier, and the hydroplanes were set to 'down'.

The boat started to dive fast, and the officer of the watch scanned the sky quickly through the periscope in order to try to get a last look at the enemy. Before the periscope dipped beneath the waves, he was able to catch a glimpse of a Liberator, and was able to note that it was several miles away, though pointing towards the boat.

The captain ordered the boat to be taken to 100 metres which was likely to be well clear of aircraft depth-charges which were normally set to explode at a shallow depth.

The actual dive was achieved in fifty seconds which was good going; and shortly afterwards, the boat was steady at 100 metres.

A little later, some dull explosions were heard, but the submarine was hardly shaken, and reports of 'no damage' came in from all compartments. The alertness of the look-out had defeated what might have been a very dangerous attack.

The next job would be to adjust the trim so that the boat would be on an even keel, and to expel the last vestiges of air from the diving-tanks.

After some minutes, and after the hydrophone operator had made a sweep round the compass and reported no contacts, the captain decided to come to periscope depth to have a look round. The hydroplanes were set to 'up', the speed of the motors was increased, and the necessary adjustments to the diving tanks were made.

Periscope depth was about twenty metres, and the periscope itself was an extremely sophisticated affair. It was trained by foot-pedals and one hand could adjust a mirror which allowed the sky to be surveyed up to an angle of 70°, while the other hand operated a compensating lever which allowed for the motion of the boat and which enabled the captain to keep pointed on to his target. There were also various shades for use in avoiding glare and the whole instrument could be warmed to prevent the misting of the mirrors. In addition, a camera or even a cine camera could be fitted to the periscope to record, for example, the last moments of a sinking ship.

In this particular case, a typical one, the captain sighted the aircraft in the distance so he decided to remain at periscope depth and keep a very sharp look-out. If the sky had been clear of aircraft, and depending on the visibility, he would have probably returned to the surface.

There was not long to wait before the first Liberator from Iceland made a sighting. The captain of aircraft E, Flying Officer Moffatt, records in his report that there was ten-tenths cloud with a base of 3,000 feet with occasional patches of cumulus cloud at 500 feet. There was a slight haze over a rough sea and the visibility was three to four miles. He also records receiving a message from the escort commander suggesting that there were plenty of U-boats astern of the convoy and that that sector should have good attention. He must have just completed one circle around the perimeter of the convoy when at 0942, when he was twelve miles astern, a U-boat was sighted two and a half miles away on the port bow. The U-boat was evidently shadowing the convoy and it was steering the same course and speed.

The aircraft immediately lost height and attacked from the port quarter of the submarine, dropping four depth-charges while the boat was still on the surface. The charges were spaced 100 feet apart, were set to explode at a shallow depth and were dropped from a height of sixty feet. Three charges were seen to drop short and the fourth was over, so the attack straddled the boat. The centre of the stick was about 100 yards short.

The submarine could not be seen for several seconds, and they thought that it had submerged, but it reappeared briefly before finally diving. The roughness of the sea quickly obliterated any traces of the attack and the smoke markers which were dropped to mark the spot were useless in these weather conditions. Five minutes after the attack a large gush of air came to the surface and a bluish tinge. The aircraft remained in the vicinity for fifteen minutes before resuming its patrol. The submarine was reported to be a Type VII of 517 tons, and three men had been seen in the

5(a). A typical freighter. These ships performed gallantly, despite their age. This particular ship is carrying a load of bombs – a very dangerous cargo. Old and slow, these vessels found difficulty in keeping station in convoy.

5(b). Tanker. This is a typical tanker of the Second World War. Tankers formed one in three of the ships sailing in convoy HX231. The hazards of life aboard these ships were many, especially when carrying a highly inflammable cargo like petrol.

6(a). The Sunderland. This flying boat came into service before the war. It performed valiantly and was the most successful anti-submarine aircraft during the first years of the war. Its endurance was too low for convoy escort in mid-ocean; in the later stages it was used mainly for patrols.

6(b). The Liberator. This fine aircraft was built in the U.S.A. as a day bomber and a number were converted to the anti-submarine role. Of these, a few were fitted with extra fuel tanks at the expense of some depth charges and became the 'Very Long Range' Liberators.

conning-tower, so it had evidently been taken completely by surprise.

The Admiralty Air Ministry Assessment Committee came, surprisingly, to the conclusion that the depth-charges had overshot and that none were in lethal range. It was reckoned, however, that one charge might have been within damaging range, so the estimate was given as 'probably slightly damaged'. Flying Officer Moffatt himself thought that the attack had been a good one and the crew were delighted. The Assessment Committee were, if anything, slightly pessimistic, because there seems no doubt from the records that Moffatt had attacked *U594*, which it will be remembered had already received some damage from a depth-charge attack by the *Vidette* on 4 April.

In his report, the U-boat captain says that water poured into the torpedo tank, more water entered one of the fuel tanks and that the pressure hull was damaged. There was also damage to a compressor, to the electric batteries and to the port shaft which was buckled. As the diving ability was seriously impaired, Kplt Mumm decided to return to harbour in order to put the boat in dock. It is difficult to criticize his decision.

E of 120 Squadron had carried out a fine attack and 'severe' rather than 'slight' damage seems a fairer assessment of the result.

Not long afterwards, T of 120 Squadron, which it will be remembered had taken a long time to find the convoy, made its first contact. For some reason or other, the normal form recording the incident has not survived, and all we know is that the aircraft attacked a U-boat at 0948 in a position well astern of the convoy. From a comparison of times, it seems that Squadron Leader Isted, the captain of the aircraft, sighted *U592* and the submarine reports that four depth-charges were dropped near her stern. The *U592* crash-dived and the charges caused much damage. The boat was badly shaken, the battery self-starter was put out of action and the compass repeaters were damaged. The damage could not be repaired, and the *U592*, which had been machine-gunned by an aircraft on the previous day, also decided to return to harbour.

The *U592* had reported the convoy to Control just before the attack, so another potential shadower had been driven off. The attack was reported to the escort commander, together with the message 'REM 2 – am still hungry' and in reply Isted was advised to pay special attention to the sector astern of the convoy during his two hours still available.

It is interesting to note that U706 heard many explosions during this period, and was thereby prevented from surfacing and using its speed to gain bearing on the convoy.

As by now, three Liberators were flying escort, it was maddening not to be able to give them accurate bearings of U-boats obtained by H/F D/F, but silence reigned supreme. X of 120 Squadron was the last of the three, and did not succeed in making any sightings until it had to leave at 1443, but, by its very presence, it helped to keep the submarines' heads down and stopped them getting into attacking positions. So what must have been a very unpleasant sortie was by no means wasted. It also sighted a lifeboat astern of the convoy which was at first taken for a U-boat. It appears that this boat must have come from some ship in another convoy; indeed, at this time, the Atlantic had many empty lifeboats scattered about as a result of the tragic losses of March.

The next attack followed quickly. Flying Officer Moffatt of E of 120 Squadron was thirty miles on the starboard quarter of the convoy. The weather conditions were unchanged and the visibility still three to four miles. A U-boat which was either well trimmed down or in the act of diving was sighted three miles on the port bow. It was steering convoy course at about 12 knots and was evidently trying to catch up. The aircraft dived to the attack, which was delivered up the track of the U-boat and the remaining two depth-charges were released, set to shallow depth. They were dropped twenty seconds after the U-boat dived and the aircrew believed that the first charge fell about thirty feet ahead of the diving swirl of the submarine. No further sign of the boat was seen and the aircraft resumed patrol after eight minutes of circling.

The Assessment Committee estimated that there was insufficient evidence of damage and they were probably right. I can find no German report of an attack at about this time and it may well have been made on U270 which complained that it was forced to dive several times by aircraft during the day.

In the convoy, things were going smoothly, and for once the weather was in favour of the defence. The *Vidette* was back in station, together with the *Loosestrife* and the *J. R. Poinsett* with their survivors, and the close screen was complete. Only the *Eclipse* was missing from the extended screen, and she was escorting the one remaining straggler.

German records show that at 1207, the *U632* claims to have torpedoed a destroyer of the *Beverley* class (the ex-American four-funnelled ships). There was no destroyer of this class with the convoy, but it would have been easy in the poor visibility to have made a mistake in identification. The position given in the *U632*'s signal was well on the starboard side of the convoy, so the most probable explanation is that the target was the *Inglefield* which was on that side of the convoy. Unfortunately, the *Inglefield*'s records have not been kept so it is impossible to check formally, but there is no record of her having made a report by signal, and an officer serving on board at the time cannot remember any incident that afternoon. To make the historians' task more difficult, the *U632* was sunk that same day, so that its War Diary is not available for checking. The only certain fact is that no escort of the convoy was hit by any torpedo!

A little later, at 1410, the *U632* reported the convoy's position, course and speed. Again, the signal was not received in any of the H/F D/F offices, and we do not know whether the report was based on a sighting or on fixes from hydrophone bearings.

At about 1400, the *U706* sighted and reported a tanker, but the range was too great and the boat was unable to get into position for attack. From the position given, it seems likely to have been the *Laurelwood* which was being shepherded by the *Eclipse*. The U-boat was not sighted nor was its signal heard by the group.

By now it was time for the first two Liberators from Iceland to return to base, leaving X of 120 Squadron to hold the fort alone. Then at 1350, G of 86 Squadron joined, followed at an hour's interval by R. from the same squadron, so that when the last air-craft of 120 Squadron left, the convoy was still strongly defended. Incidentally, the weather in Iceland was so bad that all three aircraft of 120 Squadron were diverted to Aldergrove where they each arrived safely, having completed a very successful mission, despite the weather.

86 Squadron had only just been converted to flying Liberators and was not so experienced as was 120 Squadron which had been operating these fine aircraft for several months. But they had the advantage of being based near Derry, and the aircrew paid several visits to the base, meeting officers from the escorts and going to sea with them for exercises. In addition, some sea exercises were arranged, and the squadron was learning very quickly.

In this particular case, homing procedure seemed to work smoothly, though for some reason, aircraft R took two hours less time to find the convoy than did aircraft G. Communication on convoy wave was good and both aircraft were asked to patrol round the convoy at a range of twenty to thirty miles, keeping a special look-out on the ahead and astern sectors, and coming close occasionally to check up on the position of the convoy and the waters near it.

At 1600, the escort commander decided to send off a situation report to the commander-in-chief because the aircraft had been so successful and it appeared that the U-boat signalling had died down completely. It was, I regret to say, a good example of over-confidence, because, after reporting the situation regarding the survivors of the *British Ardour* and the *Waroonga*, and the fact that the support group was in company, it remarked: 'Lack of H/F D/F activity indicates that U-boats have lost touch. Aircraft have been splendid.' The last sentence was correct, but within a few hours, plenty of H/F activity started again and it was very plain that the U-boats had not lost touch. They dived continually, both to avoid the weather and the aircraft which were so harassing them, and by listening on hydrophones they were able to keep the convoy 'fixed'.

Shortly after this signal had been sent, Flying Officer Burcher, captain of R of 86 Squadron, fully confirmed the splendid work of the aircraft. By 1618, visibility had dropped to one mile, the cloud base was down to 700 feet and the sea was still rough. While the aircraft was on the western end of the patrol, a U-boat was sighted about eighteen miles astern of the convoy. It must have been one of the shadowers.

Surprise was complete as the aircraft dived out of the clouds and sighted the submarine one mile away on the starboard bow. As in almost all these engagements, the sighting had been preceded by a radar contact, but for some reason which was probably connected with security, the use of radar (called special equipment) was not mentioned in the attack forms.

But all aircraft with the convoy had radar and there are one or two signals which indicated that an aircraft which had a failure of its radar on the way to a convoy would return to base.

The first attack was made down the submarine's track and should have been very close, but only one of the four charges which were ordered to be released, in fact dropped. It fell about fifty feet to port of the submarine and in line with the bows. The U-boat, which was a Type VII, turned hard to starboard and started to crash-dive and the aircraft had to complete a full circle before coming in for another run.

As the submarine was diving and while some of the stern was still visible, four more depth-charges were released while on a course across the port quarter of the U-boat. Observers noted that the stick entered the water with its centre about 180 feet ahead of the diving swirl and straddling the track. The charges were spaced at ninety feet and, as usual, set to shallow depth; and they were dropped from a height of only fifty feet.

It was unfortunate that the first attack had been made with only one depth-charge, but the skill needed to manoeuvre this large and heavy aircraft at a height only just above the sea in order to get in a quick second attack was beyond praise.

The aircraft circled the scene for twenty minutes and a patch of dark oil was seen in the vicinity of the explosions. A black object which might have been one of the men left in the water during the crash-dive was also sighted. The aircraft then resumed patrol.

The Assessment Committee studied the photographs of both attacks and commented that it was particularly unfortunate that the first stick had not been fully released, since the photograph was very clear and the evidence of the U-boat's position certain. The photographs of the second attack did not show the position of the diving swirl nor of the stern of the U-boat sticking out of the water, and the committee took a rather pessimistic view and estimated that the result had been 'insufficient evidence of damage'.

After the war, when fuller records were available and all the signals made by individual U-boats examined, this assessment was changed to 'probably sunk'. It seems almost certain that *U632* which had sunk the straggler *Blitar* during the night of 4/5, and which had claimed to have torpedoed a destroyer that afternoon, was sunk by aircraft R.

Although the weather was very bad, it was ideal for air anti-submarine operations. While cruising above or in the cloud cover, aircraft would be able to pick up the U-boat on their radar, diving out of the cloud and catching the submarine completely by surprise, owing to the short warning. In the stormy weather prevailing, the strong wind blowing past the conning-tower of the boat would prevent any noise of engines from being heard. The U-boats on the surface were in an unenviable position.

One more attack was made on a submarine by R of 86 Squadron before it had to return to base after four and a half hours' escort duty.

At 1847, under weather conditions similar to those of the previous affair, except that the visibility had dropped further to only three-quarters of a mile, another U-boat was sighted about thirty miles to the south of the convoy which was still steering east. It was either trimmed down or in the process of diving and was steering southwards at about 8 knots, and must, I think, have decided to break off the operation. I can find no record of the attack, and it may well have been made on *U270* which had decided to return home at about this time.

Flying Officer Burcher had only one depth-charge left. He made a very steep dive, but the initial visual sighting had been made at such a close range on the port beam that he could not get on to the track of the U-boat which was just inside his turning circle. The depth-charge was released thirteen seconds after the dive and fell about sixty yards to port of the boat and in line with the diving swirl. The Assessment Committee's estimate was correctly, it seems, that of 'no damage'.

Aircraft G of 86 Squadron, which had taken so long to find the convoy, carried out its escort duty for two hours before having to leave for its base. It was unlucky and got no sightings, but by its presence it helped to keep the U-boats away from the convoy.

R of 86 Squadron had finally to leave at 1935, just before dark, and it arrived safely at its base at Aldergrove at 2330. It had carried out a very useful and productive sortie.

In fact, the constant air cover throughout the day had been invaluable and had saved the convoy from further attacks. Communication between the escort commander and the aircraft had been good, and co-operation generally could not have been better. Although the weather had been very bad, conditions for air A/S operations had been excellent for radar-fitted aircraft. Both 120 and 86 Squadrons should have been very proud of their performance during 6 April.

In the convoy, things were quiet, with all ships and escorts in station except the *Laurelwood* and her escort the *Eclipse*. Then, just as the last aircraft left, H/F traffic was heard close in on the port bow and astern of the convoy. This came as a rude shock to the escort commander with his belief that the U-boats had lost touch. Incidentally, later that evening, the Admiralty confirmed that U-boats were still in contact.

But the silence of the day had shown yet again what a tremendous effect air cover had in keeping the U-boats down, and so preventing them from transmitting signals.

Placing the field for the night was not difficult. The wind was still strong from the south and any attack was likely to come from that direction. The visibility was poor and there was no possibility of northern lights. So the two support-group destroyers which had no asdic, were put astern and on the port quarter. The remaining escorts were evenly distributed around the convoy with those ships which had most depth-charges and most starshells remaining placed on the starboard or southern side.

Just after dark, the usual deceptive alteration of course was made, this time to starboard; although there is no firm evidence, it seems to have been successful. Anyhow, no U-boat attacked during the night, and no radar contacts were picked up. The only disturbance was when two ships of the convoy started to fire at each other; but it was not possible to see which ships were responsible in the poor weather, and nothing more was heard of the incident. Probably two ships came too close and a nervous gunner on one let fly at what he thought was a submarine!

There was much H/F signalling near the convoy throughout the night and the ships of the extended screen investigated one or two possible U-boats, but nothing was found. It was necessary also to keep alert constantly, as it was not known when an attack might come, so that few captains got much sleep.

It came as a welcome relief when dawn broke and it was realized that despite the sizable numbers of submarines still in contact, none had been successful. The main reason for this was a combination of circumstances: the defeat of the attacks on the night before; the constant harassment received from aircraft during the day; the barrier of the outer screen; and finally the poor visibility.

At 1849 on 6 April, the Admiralty, presumably encouraged by the escort commander's signal about the U-boats having lost touch, gave him the option of sending the support group to another convoy – SC125 – next day, 7 April, if no further attacks were made. After some discussion with the senior officer, it was decided that the support group should remain with the convoy until noon on 7 April, when the situation should be clearer.

However, at 0644 on 7 April, the Admiralty, which had now realized that the pack was still in contact, cancelled its signal and ordered the support group to remain with convoy HX231.

From the German records, there is no doubt as to how contact was maintained in such poor visibility. U260 reported that it had kept touch for four hours by hydrophone fixes, and U563 also signalled that four times during the night it had obtained a fix by the same means.

There were still eight boats operating against the convoy.

The U-boat headquarters War Diary records an attack during

the night by the *U270*, but this must be a mistake as the details of the attack are exactly similar to one reported the night before by the *U270*. It is certain that no attempt was made during the night of 6/7.

It appears that the captains of the members of Group *Löwenherz* were beginning to lose heart, as a determined effort should have resulted in at least one attack on the convoy.

# 9

# From the Fourth Day
# Until the End of the Convoy Passage

During the night 6/7 April, U-boat headquarters instructed the remaining boats of Group *Löwenherz* to overtake the convoy during darkness in order to be able to make attacks submerged from ahead after daylight. The boats were also informed, correctly it turned out, that the convoy would pass just south of the Rockall Bank on a course of 100°, bound for the North Channel.

During the night, the *Tay, Inglefield* and *Icarus* heard a considerable amount of H/F traffic and got some bearings on ground-wave. This must have been acknowledgement of instructions and information about the state of fuel and torpedoes and other important logistical matters.

At dawn on 7 April, the escort commander strengthened the positions ahead and on the bow of the convoy by a rearrangement designed to deal with the expected daylight attack, but as far as the escort knew, nothing happened. In fact, *U563* reports having been chased by an escort between 0645 and 0714, but the ship concerned, which from the position given was likely to have been the *Inglefield*, was quite unaware of the submarine's presence and was carrying out her normal zigzag.

Either the U-boats had failed to get ahead of the convoy during the night or else the nerves of the captains were beginning to shake.

The convoy was now complete, for the *Laurelwood* had arrived, having made good repairs to her engines which had caused the straggling. It was then possible to put the *Eclipse* on the extended screen.

Spirits in the escort began to rise for not only did the weather, while vile for ships, continue to be admirable for anti-submarine operations from the air, but a full flying programme had been arranged. If conditions at base allowed the aircraft to take off, they were in for a busy time.

With Iceland well astern, 120 Squadron had been relieved of the responsibility of looking after the convoy and was covering another one, farther to the west. Instead, 86 Squadron was to take over the close escort. In addition 206 Squadron of Fortress aircraft, stationed in Scotland, was to carry out a parallel sweep patrol to the south of the convoy and three Catalinas of 84 (U.S.N.) Squadron were also instructed to help, but only two managed to take off and they both had to return to base owing to the appalling weather.

Let us take the parallel sweep first. It was carried out by four Fortresses, and the northern one just sighted the convoy on two occasions. It was not uneventful. At 1546, C of 206 Squadron, commanded by Flying Officer Clark, attacked a U-boat about sixty miles south of the convoy. Unfortunately, no records exist of the attack on either side and no comment can be made. In addition aircraft D, whose captain was Flying Officer Cowie, sighted a lifeboat with survivors on board and dropped food. Next day, this lifeboat was to be picked up by the *Eclipse*, whose search was helped by aircraft D's report of the boat's position. The boat came from the torpedoed *Blitar*.

But to the convoy, the most important sortie was by the Liberator of 86 Squadron, which was to provide the close escort. Aircraft W, commanded by Flight-Lieutenant E. C. Hammond, took off at 0120 from Aldergrove and started homing procedure at 0605. Due to the fact that the signal warning the ships of the details of the times of setting radio watch had arrived too late, the homing was not successful, but Hammond succeeded in finding the convoy at 0805. The escort commander gave instructions for a patrol around the convoy at a distance of about ten miles with special attention to the sector ahead, where some signalling had been heard. He also briefed the aircraft on the situation generally and in particular on the position of the two ships on the extended screen.

The weather was ideal for the job, though difficult for flying and unpleasant for surface ships. The cloud was again ten-tenths, and the base was as low as 200 feet with some patches of cloud down to sea-level. The visibility was about two miles.

At 0919, Flight-Lieutenant Hammond sighted a U-boat on the surface right ahead of the aircraft and only one mile away. It was steering convoy course and speed, which was little south of east at 9 knots, and was certainly in contact, being only five miles north-west of the convoy.

An attack was immediately made down the U-boat's track, but all four depth-charges failed to release and a great chance was missed. The heavy Liberator was then hauled round in a steep turn, first to port and then to starboard and delivered a second attack, this time up the U-boat's track.

Four depth-charges exploded, set to shallow and spaced at 100 feet, twenty seconds after the boat had dived. Observers noted that the first charge entered the water just astern of the diving swirl and another about 170 feet ahead of the apex of the swirl, while the last fell some 200 feet ahead.

When the aircraft circled the scene three minutes later all traces of the swirl and the explosions had vanished in the rough sea, but two patches of oil were sighted. Greenish streaks were also seen and the oil patches grew in size. The aircraft remained in the vicinity for thirty minutes but no further traces were seen.

The Assessment Committee's report is worth quoting in some detail, as it gives some indication of the difficulty of its task. After regretting the Liberator's failure to drop charges during the first attack which proved to have been due to a mistake in drill by a member of the aircrew, it went on to say:

'There were no photographs of the attack and it is our experience that we are unable to place full reliance on descriptions of oil patches seen by members of the crew and reported to be in the position where the attacks were made.

'Intelligence may come to hand in the future to give us some indication of the damage caused to U-boats during the attack on convoy HX231. On the present report, although damage is distinctly possible, the attack must be assessed as "insufficient evidence of damage".'

*U563* reports that it was attacked at exactly the same time as W of 86 Squadron's activities and said that the depth-charges fell astern of the boat without causing damage. *U563*'s diary also includes the fact that one man was left in the water when the boat crash-dived, that he had no life-jacket and could not be found when the boat surfaced later. The committee's assessment seems to have been accurate.

A signal from the Admiralty during the forenoon made plain that there were still U-boats ahead of the convoy, though the group's own H/F D/F bearings also indicated that most of the boats still in touch were astern.

The next attack, again by Flight-Lieutenant Hammond of aircraft W, came at 1234. The weather conditions were similar to those during the first attack and the submarine was sighted, with decks awash, and obviously just diving, dead ahead at a range of a mile and a half.

It was steering for the convoy from a position about fourteen miles on the starboard quarter. The conning-tower disappeared at a range of one mile and the remaining two depth-charges were released twenty-five seconds after the boat had dived. The crew reported that the depth-charges exploded along the U-boat's track with the first charge going off about 200 feet ahead of the diving swirl.

The Assessment Committee agreed that the attack was inaccurate and missed well astern of the U-boat. No signs of damage were seen, and after five minutes of circling the spot, aircraft W resumed patrol.

This was not to be aircraft W's last encounter with the enemy in the course of a very busy sortie. It had to return to base at 1554, and shortly afterwards at 1612, it sighted yet another U-boat, this time some way ahead of the convoy. There were no depth-charges left, so Flight-Lieutenant Hammond dived at the submarine and machine-gunned the conning-tower, so forcing the boat, which did not return the fire, to crash-dive. Aircraft W landed safely at Aldergrove after sixteen hours in the air.

The next aircraft, X of 86 Squadron, commanded by Flying Officer Walker, arrived only ten minutes after aircraft W had left, so there was little gap in the coverage. Homing procedure had been excellent and only three and a half hours had been taken from leaving base and meeting the convoy.

The first task ordered was to investigate an H/F D/F bearing, signalled by the escort commander, but nothing was seen, and the normal circuit patrol which, with a large convoy like HX231, took about an hour to carry out, was started.

At 1710, the aircraft was sent out to investigate another H/F D/F bearing which in this case proved fruitful. By now, the visibility was only half a mile with patches of very low cloud and as the aircraft emerged from the clouds, it sighted a submarine which was in the act of diving, on a course parallel to the convoy which was still steering a little south of east. It was ten miles to the south of the convoy and not far from the extended screen.

The aircraft which had sighted the submarine dead ahead had little time to manœuvre, so close was the initial sighting, but it succeeded in attacking only 30° off track from the starboard side.

Five seconds after the conning-tower had disappeared and while a few feet of the stern were still visible, five depth-charges were dropped at the usual settings. The aircrew believed that the first charge exploded on the edge of the diving swirl but that the remainder overshot. The escort commander had sent the *Inglefield* to the scene as soon as the attack had been reported, and when the destroyer was sighted, the aircraft resumed patrol. The *Inglefield* made a thorough A/S search of the area but found nothing.

The Assessment Committee agreed that only one depth-charge could have fallen within a dangerous distance of the boat, but reckoned that it may well have been carried forward out of lethal range; and the estimate was 'insufficient evidence of damage'. I can find no report of this attack in the German records.

This was the last air attack of the day and aircraft X remained with the convoy until dusk, continuing to do useful work by keeping the U-boats away from the convoy. Again it had been a great day for aircraft, though the escort commander remarked in his report that communications had not been so good as during the two previous days.

The evidence of U-boat headquarters is conclusive and reads:

'No further reports received on 7 April regarding the convoy. Positions of two destroyers [these must have been the two on the extended screen] only were reported. Since the air cover in the coastal area is very strong and boats are continually bombed, the operation was broken off on the evening of the seventh.'

In fact, the convoy had hardly reached the coastal area, but it was now in range of the shorter-legged aircraft like the Sunderlands and it was possible to lay on very strong air escort.

That evening, the Admiralty again gave the escort commander the option of dispensing with the services of the support group. Of course, he was quite unaware that the operations against the convoy had been called off, but after a discussion with the senior officer, it was agreed that the support group would leave at dawn unless something special happened. Three ships would then, in accordance with Admiralty instructions, sweep for 100 miles down the track astern of the convoy before joining convoy SC125, while the *Eclipse* was ordered to search for the lifeboat full of survivors which had been reported earlier by aircraft.

It was just as well that the support group stayed for the night, because before midnight, at 2258, the *Inglefield*, which was then on the starboard quarter of the convoy picked up a radar contact and fired a star-shell, in the light of which a submarine was sighted. All this roused some excitement in the convoy where the escorts could see the illumination. The *Inglefield's* U-boat dived promptly, but no asdic contact was obtained and so depth-charges were dropped in the estimated position of the boat and a search was started. After some time, a patch of oil was sighted, but again with no asdic contact, and after an hour's search, the ship resumed station. As has been noted already, no records from the *Inglefield* survive, and this account is taken from the signal records of the escorts of B7 Group, and from the memory of an officer who was aboard at the time.

The night continued to be busy. Just after midnight, a U-boat was heard signalling close ahead of the convoy and ships were warned to be especially alert. It was probably one of the boats which had not yet received the signal to break off the operation.

Shortly afterwards, the *Tay* sighted what might have been red flares in the convoy, and the escort commander, fearing another torpedoing, asked all concerned whether they had anything to report.

The replies 'nothing to report' came in quickly and the tension subsided. Subsequently it appeared that one of the ships must have hoisted her 'not under control' lights, which consisted of two red lights vertically, for a short time and that these were mistaken for rockets.

The rest of the night was uneventful, with the German signalling getting less and less as U-boats acknowledged the orders to break away.

The support group left at dawn, after mutual exchanges of goodwill, and at about this time, the convoy was passing across the Rockall Bank, not far from Rockall itself. It was now at last clear that the worst was over, and the escort commander sent off a long report on the general situation, going also into such domestic detail as asking for tugs to meet two ships with poor steering, and for the *Vidette* which had leaking oil-fuel tanks to be docked on arrival.

A Sunderland aircraft, O of 201 Squadron, gave useful escort for six hours from dawn, and the report stresses that communication and co-operation were excellent. But no U-boats could be produced, and the flying-boat had a quiet sortie.

There was a good deal of air activity in the general direction of the convoy as well; and during the day, Sunderland E of 423 Squadron commanded by Pilot Officer Bishop sighted a submarine some miles astern. This must have been one of the survivors of the pack going off to its next assignment. The aircraft made what should have been a perfect attack, but owing to faulty cockpit drill, the depth-charges were dropped set to 'safe' and no damage was done.

In addition, Sunderland N of 228 Squadron, commanded by Flight-Lieutenant Briscoe, sighted the *Blitar*'s lifeboat, which had been reported by a Fortress the day before. The captain asked permission from base to land on the water to take off survivors, but the request was refused as the sea and swell were still high. An

7. Depth charge attack on a U-boat. The U-boat, which is still fully surfaced, is almost hidden by the plumes of the depth charge explosions which straddled the boat. At the start of the war, aircraft depth charges were set to explode at one hundred feet, but after operational research, all aircraft depth charge settings were changed to 25 feet. There was an immediate increase in the number of kills per attack. This photograph shows an excellent attack which sank the U-boat.

8. Attack on U-boat with machine guns. Possibly, the aircraft had expended all its depth charges before sighting this U-boat and is making a determined attack with machine guns. In contests between aircraft and the A.A. guns of U-boats, the aircraft was very vulnerable and many were shot down.

accurate position was passed to the *Eclipse*, and she picked up the survivors that same day (see Chapter 10).

Later that afternoon, the convoy was reckoned to be safe from further attack, so the section destined for Iceland was detached, escorted initially by the *Pink* until the proper Iceland escort of a trawler took over. The Loch Ewe section, bound for the convoy assembly anchorage in the west of Scotland was the next to go, escorted by the *Alisma* and the commodore started to sort out the convoy into the three long lines: one for the Clyde section; one for the Liverpool section; and the right-hand line for the section which went on to Belfast and Milford Haven.

Next day, 9 April, at 1600 (B.S.T.), the local escort which was a trawler took over responsibility for the safety of the convoy, and the *Tay*, the *Vidette*, the *Loosestrife* and the *Snowflake*, both the latter with survivors on board, proceeded up the River Foyle to Derry where they arrived before dark.

On leaving, the group was given the memorable sight of these three long lines of heavily laden ships steering for the North Channel between Scotland and Ireland against the background of the grey cliffs and green fields of Ulster. It was a most satisfactory finish to what had sometimes seemed to be a passage which would never come to an end.

Some ships had become old friends like the *Tyndareus*, the ideal flagship for the commodore which had always been alert and cheerful, and the *J. R. Poinsett* which had so bravely stopped to rescue some of the *Waroonga* survivors. Some others, like the *Erin*, the *Empire Dickens* and the *British Confidence*, had gained the commodore's commendation for excellent station-keeping under trying conditions.

There were one or two ships which had not been very popular, like the *Aruba* with her eccentric steering and the *Thomas Sumpter* which had been so lucky to survive breaking out of the convoy during the first night's attacks. But the great thing was that they had arrived safely, and we mourned the certain loss of only three ships in convoy and the probable loss of three others while straggling or after having broken away.

The intricate machinery of the organization which controlled

119

the routing of merchant ships now took over. Some ships would go straight to their destination, some would immediately join coastal convoys and some would wait at assembly anchorages for a convenient coastal convoy to take them to their eventual unloading port. It was a remarkable organization, experienced by years of war, and it always seemed a marvel that it worked so well. It was flexible too, and destinations could be changed at short notice if, for example, a port was short of space due to an air raid, or due to what I regret sometimes happened even in wartime, a strike.

The *Snowflake* and the *Loosestrife* landed their survivors on arrival at Derry that evening. Each ship reported how helpful the men had been. Extra look-outs had been posted, the engineers had made themselves available for odd jobs and there had been offers to clean and paint. The survivors' morale remained high throughout and they were a credit to the Merchant Navy. The captain of the *Waroonga* expressed the general feeling as he walked down the gangway. 'Now,' he said, 'I shall have to see about getting another ship.'

Everyone in the escorts was very tired, but feeling well satisfied that after a shaky start, the group had lost so few ships against a most formidable opposition. There was one final battle to be fought: the battle of the reports which had to be quickly finished and handed in to the staff ashore. Otherwise it was not possible to hold, before the group next sailed on convoy duty, a conference of all concerned where the lessons could be discussed, the mistakes analysed and new exercises designed to put things right where they had gone wrong.

Some of the aircrew who had escorted the group in aircraft from 86 Squadron would also be present at the conference and some valuable results always emerged from these meetings. Not only did the captains get together, but the radio operators of ships and aircraft were able to exchange experiences and in some cases arrange for exercises to be held. We were never satisfied, and sought improvement in every aspect of convoy escort work.

# 10

# The Fate of the Survivors

The stories of the survivors of the ships which were torpedoed and sunk from HX231 are highly dramatic and provide a record which heightens the appreciation of man's capacity for self-sacrifice and for survival under dreadful conditions. The story of the two ships from which no one was rescued is truly tragic.

Throughout the ordeals of the men in the lifeboats, the weather was uniformly bad: sometimes dangerously rough, sometimes slightly eased when the efforts to keep the boats afloat could be relaxed. It was very cold, and many of the men had been in the sea before reaching the boats; the remainder were soon soaked with spray and with the water in the bottom of the boats.

It is better not to dwell too long on the fate of the crew of the Swedish *Vaarlaren*, which was hit at 0109 on 5 April, soon after leaving the convoy, and which sank in seven minutes. The *U229* (Oblt Schetelig) reported that one boat got away before the ship sank stern first, but there is no evidence that any of the crew reached it. Nothing was seen or heard of the boat again. The ship never transmitted a distress call and so the escort commander did not know that she had been torpedoed. In any case, as she had broken away from the convoy without orders and was some miles away, he could not have spared an escort to look for her.

The experience of the men in the *Vaarlaren*'s boat, if any reached it, defy the imagination and it can only be hoped that their end was peaceful. All accounts of such deaths in other boats provide good hope that this was so. The full crew of the ship amounted to thirty-seven men and one woman. The tragedy was even sharper as Sweden was neutral and there was no obligation for these men and women to fight for the freedom of the world as they so valiantly did.

·     ·     ·     ·     ·

The crew of the *British Ardour*, owned by the British Petroleum Company, had a lucky escape. When the torpedo struck them on the port side at 1215 on 5 April, the explosion covered the forward part of the ship and the bridge with oil which promptly caught fire.

The master, Captain Copeman, tried hard to get to the confidential books, but he was beaten back by the flames. The ship seemed to be settling by the bows and the fire was evidently completely out of control, so he decided to order 'abandon ship', using the two lifeboats near the stern which were the only ones available after the explosion. Of the crew of fifty-four, only a look-out, A.B. Etherington, and the helmsman, A.B. Tolman, were injured, neither seriously. The rest were unharmed.

After laying off the ship for an hour and a half, it became plain that the fire was increasing its grip, and that reboarding, which had been suggested by the escort commander, was impossible. So the crew were taken aboard the corvette *Snowflake* which, with the *Vidette*, then tried to sink the wreck, using both guns and depth-charges. Even a passing Liberator, P of 120 Squadron, was called in to help and dropped two depth-charges near the tanker; but when at 1600 the *Snowflake* had to leave in order to rejoin the convoy before dark, the ship was burning fiercely and still lying low in the water, bows down.

The survivors were very crowded in the small corvette, and they lived through an exciting night when so many attacks on the convoy were beaten off and when the crump of depth-charges and the thunder of guns were constantly heard. But they were warm and dry, with plenty of food and water, and they adjudged themselves lucky.

The *Waroonga*, of the British India Company it will be remembered, had sturdily remained in station in the convoy until early on 6 April, thirty-six hours after being torpedoed. Then the increasingly rough seas which rose up during the night caused the bulkheads to give way. The pumps could not compete, and the ship began to sink by the stern. The master, Captain C. C. Taylor, ordered the engines to be stopped, warned the corvette *Loosestrife* which had been detailed to keep guard on the *Waroonga* and then gave the order to abandon ship.

Despite the weather, six boats were safely lowered, two others having been smashed by the seas; but No. 4 boat, which was on the lee side, found difficulty in getting away from the ship which was drifting fast down upon it, caught its keel in the rail of the *Waroonga* and capsized. Three army gunners and a cadet managed to climb back aboard and found a raft from which they were later rescued; but most of the occupants were drowned, and out of a total of nineteen men lost, fourteen were in No. 4 boat.

The captain, who was the last to leave, jumped into No. 2 boat, which was also having great difficulty in getting away from the drifting ship. But owing mainly to the strength of Gunner Allingham, and after breaking five oars while shoving off, they got clear and took twenty-three men to safety.

The *Loosestrife* and an American merchant ship, the *J. R. Poinsett* (Captain T. A. Morasson), rescued all the men in the boats while the *Vidette* screened the stopped ships from U-boat attack. The corvette took seventy-two men and the *Poinsett* forty-one. Conditions were difficult and both ships showed excellent seamanship during the operation. The *Loosestrife* then decided to sink the wreck, but she was saved the trouble as the *Waroonga* sank at 0650, only one hour after having been abandoned.

The master reported very favourably on the conduct of the European crew and mentioned particularly the chief officer, Mr H. C. Turner and the chief engineer, Mr S. Button, for their coolness during the emergency. Unhappily, the chief engineer was drowned in No. 4 boat. Captain Taylor also mentioned Cadet Logie, who took charge of a boat with great efficiency, and Gunner Allingham for outstanding conduct and strength.

It is impossible to speak too highly of the conduct of the men of the *Waroonga*. They steamed their ship with great bravery for thirty-six hours when there was a hole in the side through which a car could have been driven. They left the ship only at the last moment, and they were ill-rewarded by the loss of nineteen men by drowning. The *Loosestrife* mentions their excellent behaviour on board and the work which they voluntarily carried out. Captain Taylor and his chief officer are still alive today.

The *Blitar* of the Rotterdam Lloyd line had deliberately broken out of the convoy during the attacks of the evening of 4 April. After the *Shillong* and the *Waroonga* had been hit, a council of war had decided, strongly advised by the captain, that the ship would be safer clear of the convoy and that they stood a better chance sailing independently at 13 knots than with the convoy at 9. The captain was to change his mind later that day, but it was too late!

The *Blitar* left the convoy at 2305 and set a zigzag course for Ireland at her best speed. But soon after dawn she was sighted and followed by *U229* (Oblt Schetelig) which eventually reached a position to fire from submerged at 1055. The torpedo missed and the submarine surfaced on the port quarter of the *Blitar* and engaged her with gunfire at a range of 6,000 yards. Owing to the movement of the U-boat, the fire was not accurate. The *Blitar* returned the fire at once with several rounds which seemed to fall close but which the *U229* reports were short. Indeed the *Blitar*'s crew believed that they had forced the submarine to dive, leaving men in the water. What had happened, however, was that the U-boat's gun had jammed after only six rounds and the engagement had been broken off. The *Blitar* had won the first round.

It was then that Captain Knip decided that he would rejoin the convoy after dark, as he now believed that they had a better chance of being picked up if torpedoed in convoy. But it was too late, for there were two more submarines on the *Blitar*'s track. The *U632* sighted her at 1155 and started a long pursuit which culminated in the firing of two torpedoes at 1839. Both missed and the *U632* took up the chase again with the object of making another attempt.

But meanwhile, at 1605, the *U631* had sighted the *Blitar* as well, and also made contact with the *U632* which was in the vicinity. By 2003, the *U631* was also in position to attack and fired two torpedoes, both of which missed – the cause being logged as 'incorrect setting'. So the submarine set course to get in position for yet another attack.

So we now have Krüger in *U631* and Karpf in *U632* both anxious to fire. But Karpf had called Control and asked permission to fire a pattern-running torpedo (called F.A.T.). Control had agreed and so *U631* had to hold off from the attack and dive deep to avoid any danger from the pattern runner.

*U632*'s F.A.T. torpedo hit the *Blitar* at 2136 on the starboard side. The survivors reported that the four double boilers exploded, and that the ship 'looked as if hell had broken out'. Great sheets of flame rose from the upper deck and wreckage was thrown in the air. There were shouts from the injured but no panic, and although the lights went out, the emergency lamps worked well, and as the ship started to settle, men began to lower the boats.

On the starboard side, No. 1 boat was smashed and destroyed by the explosion, and No. 3 boat's davits were twisted which made lowering the boat very difficult. After great efforts, the crew got the boat into the water; but simultaneously, *U632* fired another torpedo which hit near No. 3 boat, destroyed it and killed most of the crew. This was at 2230, and shortly afterwards the *Blitar* sank.

On the port side, No. 2 boat under the chief officer, Mr De Haan, got away safely with thirty-four men aboard, the captain jumping in at the last moment. No. 4 boat, under the fourth officer, also succeeded in getting away with fifteen men aboard only. But the reserve boat, No. 6, which was near the stern, had considerable trouble in getting clear when the ship started to sink, and axes and knives had to be used. Some damage was done before the boat, under the second officer, got clear with sixteen men aboard.

Three boats had thus got safely away, and while they were trying to pick up men from the water, a submarine was heard in the darkness, and the *U631*, which had not fired the fatal torpedoes, approached. No. 6 boat was first investigated, but the occupants hid under the thwarts and so persuaded the submarine that the boat was empty. So Krüger set off for No. 2 boat and asked in English, 'Where are the captain and the chief officer?' But as neither officer was wearing uniform to be distinguished from the rest, the answer 'Don't know' was given.

Krüger then said, 'Come alongside or I shoot,' and when the efforts to get the boat to the submarine failed owing to the seas, he shouted, 'Row for your lives, I give you five or ten minutes'. Eventually the U-boat ordered one of the men from No. 2 boat to jump into the water and swim to the submarine; and Captain Knip, still affirming that he was an Able Seaman, set off and was hauled aboard the U-boat. Here he refused to give any more information than that the ship had some hides in her cargo; he continued to deny vehemently that he was an officer, and the Germans obtained remarkably little information from this courageous man.

The U-boat then informed the boats that the man was being released and Captain Knip was pushed into the water. The wind and sea were so strong that the boats were unable to make any headway towards him, and they had the agonizing experience of seing the red light on his life-jacket disappear and his shouts die away. There died a brave man.

Krüger excused himself by saying that the submarine had next to proceed to a secret rendezvous with a 'Milch Cow' tanker, and that no prisoners were allowed on board during the operation of fuelling. But he could easily have dropped Captain Knip nearer to the boats and ensured that he was picked up. His conduct deserved trial for crimes against humanity at Nuremberg, but he did not survive to face his accusers. It was a suitable retribution that *U631* was sunk by a member of B7 Group, the *Sunflower*, in October 1943.

Let us now take up the story of No. 2 and No. 4 boats under the chief and second officers. Rough weather prevented them from hoisting sails during the first night, and they had to wait until daylight. It was very cold and miserable, the men were wet, and some Javanese and Chinese died of exposure. Both boats were determined to sail to Scotland, which they judged was about 600 miles away, and at dawn the sails were hoisted and course was set; but No. 2 boat was heavier than No. 4, and sailed more slowly, and the two soon became separated. So we continue with the story of No. 2 boat with Chief Officer de Haan.

That first night, on April, the boat had lain to a sea anchor. The first anchor had failed and they had to construct another, which worked better. The boat had been damaged when leaving the ship, and was leaking. The small hand-pump did not work, and they had to bale out, removing over 100 buckets of water every hour.

At dawn on 6 April, they hoisted the sails, having difficulty in keeping on a course due to the heavy sea. From time to time they would transmit an S.O.S. emessage on the mergency radio set, but these signals were never received by any station. The routine of sailing by day and heaving to during the night continued throughout 7, 8 and 9 April, but on 7 April, a Fortress aircraft B of 206 Squadron sighted No. 2 boat and dropped three packages of food, two of which were picked up by the boat. The food and the renewed hope of rescue encouraged the men who were beginning to wonder if they would survive.

But there were three days still to endure and the men became depressed, especially as during the night of 8/9 April the Chinese drank a large part of the water ration. However, the weather then started to improve for the first time and they were able to continue sailing during the night.

On 10 April, nearly five days after the *Blitar* had sunk, the masts and funnels of a destroyer were seen on the horizon. Verey lights were fired to attract attention, and very soon all the occupants of No. 2 boat were aboard the Canadian destroyer *Restigouche* (HOO). They were treated by the doctor, given baths and clean clothes and were settled down to a badly needed sleep. The *Restigouche* was part of C4 group, escorting convoy ON177; and another ship of the group, the British frigate *Trent* (K243) picked up No. 4 boat's occupants only three hours later.

A total of thirty-eight survivors was landed at St John's, Newfoundland, on 18 April and all had recovered completely from their ordeal. Indeed, Chief Officer de Haan had lectured about their experience to the crew of the *Restigouche* while she was still at sea. The determination and courage of these men was tremendous. When they were picked up, they still had 300 miles to sail and I believe that they would have done it.

No. 6 boat, under the fourth officer, Mr Groeneveld, adopted a very different policy. The sixteen men, among whom were several British gunners, spent the days keeping as dry and warm as possible. They rigged a shelter of sails in the stern under which three would sit at a time for four-hour spells while they waited for rescue. The food and the water were carefully rationed, and the men lay still, without making any effort to reach land.

On the evening of 7 April, they were sighted by a Flying Fortress aircraft (D of 206 Squadron) commanded by Flying Officer Cowie, which reported their position to base and the destroyer *Eclipse* was detached from the Fourth Support Group to search for the boat.

On the next morning, 8 April, a Sunderland flying boat (N of 228 Squadron), commanded by Flight-Lieutenant R. Briscoe, sighted the lifeboat and circled it for several minutes. It will be remembered that Briscoe asked permission to land and pick up the survivors; but the sea and swell were still high, the operation would have been hazardous and his request was refused by base.

The position of the boat was again passed to the *Eclipse* by radio and that evening at 2043, the destroyer picked up the sixteen survivors from No. 6 boat and took them to Iceland.

In the end, by the exercise of courage, patience and endurance, fifty-four men had been saved. Twenty-six, including Captain Knip, had died. It had taken three German submarines several rounds of ammunition and a total of eight torpedoes before the *Blitar* had been eventually sunk: a remarkable story of defence and defiance.

There are several aspects of the sinking of the American tanker *Sunoil*, lost without the rescue of a single survior, which have proved impossible yet to resolve. The only certain facts are that the ship was torpedoed at about 1800 on 5 April, after a long chase; that she must have sunk quite quickly; and that opportunities probably occurred for boats to get away, but that nothing was seen of her despite a search. The fate of the crew, like that of the *Vaarlaren*, can be imagined only with horror.

The *Sunoil* (No. 45) had started to drop astern of the convoy during the early morning of 5 April, probably just after the last of the night attacks had been beaten off by the *Alisma* at 0300. The tanker was the last ship in the fourth column, on the left-hand side of the convoy. Her absence was not immediately noticed, though in a signal to the Admiralty at 0610, the escort commander had reported that she was straggling.

At 0400, the *U563* commanded by Kplt Hartmann, tried to get into position between the convoy and the *Sunoil* but failed. At 0530, he reports having been forced to dive by an escort, but he surfaced again at 0615 and again sighted the *Sunoil* which was by now zigzagging.

He pursued her until he was in a position to fire and at 0745, he attacked with three torpedoes, only one of which hit. The tanker replied with accurate machine-gun fire which forced the submarine to dive again.

The *U563* reports that an escort then came to the help of the tanker and dropped two depth-charges. The U-boat hydroplanes had jammed in the 'surface' position and it was found very difficult to dive, the conning-tower remaining above the water for some time. The captain of *U563*, by listening on hydrophones, estimated that the speed of the tanker's engines was seventy-four revolutions per minute, giving some 7 knots, and he broke off the chase.

At 0800, the *Sunoil* broadcast a distress signal which was received by the escort commander and by shore radio stations, and the destroyer *Vidette* was sent astern to her assistance, with firm instructions to return to the convoy before dark.

The inexplicable feature of the U-boat's report is that there is no record of any escort having been in the vicinity of the *Sunoil* during this engagement. The only ship of B7 Group which was not with the convoy at the time was the *Pink*, which was returning from an unsuccessful search for the survivors of the *Shillong*. But her records show no trace that she even sighted the *Sunoil*, let alone defended her from attack, and by 0800 when the *Sunoil* was first torpedoed the *Pink* cannot have been more than six miles astern of the convoy, which she rejoined at 0900.

I combed the records to see if any other ship could possibly have been operating in the vicinity, but found no sign. So I got into touch with Hartman in Germany, who remembers the incident clearly. He says that visibility was poor and that he did not actually sight any escort near the *Sunoil*, but that two explosions were heard.

The most likely explanation must be therefore that the two explosions were caused by the two torpedoes, which missed the *Sunoil*, detonating at the end of their run. Hartmann then assumed that an escort had dropped depth-charges.

Yet another submarine, the *U168*, commanded by Kplt Pich, also reports sighting the tanker at the same time as the *U563* and in about the same position, and records that an escort was in the vicinity. It seems that Pich made the same mistake as Hartmann in assuming that the *Sunoil* had been escorted.

The *U168* also tried to attack the tanker, and failed. Surprisingly, the log makes no mention of the *U563*'s successful attack.

The whole story of this engagement illustrates, I think, the difficulty of identification in low visibility and the inevitable confusion when two U-boats, unknown to each other, were trying to sink the same ship. Pich records in his log that he was frustrated by the tanker's zigzags. In any case, compared with those of most other U-boat captains, Pich's reports were models of brevity which probably accounts for his omission of the *U563*'s successful attack.

Later on, at 1102, the contact keeper, *U530*, reports having sighted a tanker which could only have been the *Sunoil*. She must have continued to steam doggedly on, for at 1235, the *U572* (Oblt Kummetat) also sighted her, though the submarine did not get close enough to attack. The *Sunoil*, which must have been keeping a good look-out, saw the *U572* and transmitted another distress signal.

Eventually, the end came. The *U530* which had been following the tanker for seven hours fired, at 1800, three torpedoes, one of which hit. The log records that two more torpedoes were needed to finish off the ship. The time of this last attack is corroborated by the *U572* which reports having heard three explosions at 1800 in the approximate position given by *U530*.

Nothing more was heard or seen of the tanker. No further

distress signal was received and it must be assumed that the radio office was damaged by the final torpedoing. It was tragic that this fine ship which took the combined efforts of four submarines finally to sink her, should have left no survivors of her brave defence.

Unfortunately the *Vidette* found no trace of her and had to abandon the search and return to the convoy. This gives yet another example of the appalling decisions which had to be taken to recall escorts to the convoy in order to defend it against further attack: decisions which were taken in the certainty that men were struggling for their lives in the water astern.

As has already been recounted, the P & O steamer *Shillong* (No. 121) was the leading ship of the twelfth column and was loaded with over 4,000 tons of zinc and 3,000 tons of wheat. When she was struck by the torpedo in the engine-room on the port side, she stopped at once. The bridge and radio office were wrecked by blast, but there were no casualties.

The senior survivor was Cadet (Apprentice) David Clowe and the rest of this narrative is based on his report, amplified by the account of Cadet A. Moore, also one of the seven survivors.

The two lifeboats on the port side had been damaged by heavy seas and ice when the ship was south of Newfoundland, before the ocean escort had joined. The mainmast had also broken and the ship had stopped for repairs and to lash down the lifeboats. When they rejoined the convoy the commodore asked the *Shillong* if they wished to return to harbour, but the master had decided to press on. It must have been an agonizing decision to take and it proved to be tragically wrong; but who could blame a man who knew how desperately his cargo was needed in Britain? There was not room for all the crew in the two remaining boats, and so rafts were prepared ready for easy launching in emergency.

After the torpedoing, the two boats on the starboard side were lowered, but the motor-boat which also contained the emergency radio set, capsized on hitting the water, and could not be righted. This left one boat, with a nominal capacity of thirty-two men, to take seventy-eight.

Only one raft survived and about twenty-four men climbed on to it, or hung on to its lines from the water. There were thirty-three survivors in the lifeboat, and the remaining eleven men perished in the water. The ship sank quickly and soon afterwards, an escort, the *Tay*, passed the raft with some men in the water nearby, and shouted encouragement, promising to return later, which cheered them up.

The lifeboat lay to a sea anchor throughout the night, the sea was rough and several dead bodies in their life-jackets were encountered. It was also very cold and the senior radio officer died during the hours of darkness.

The raft had capsized three times during the night, and on each occasion, men had been swept off and drowned. Only five out of twenty-four were left, and the captain, the chief officer and the third officer were among those who died. Cadet Moore and the third engineer had lived, and when light came they sighted the lifeboat about a mile away. They paddled hard towards the boat which also made great effort to move towards them, but it was slow work in the heavy seas and several hours passed before the five men were able to transfer to the boat. Moore writes of the self-sacrifice of Cadet Francis who wore himself out while helping others in the water and who died on the raft from exposure and fatigue.

Of the thirty-eight men now in the boat, there were eleven British and twenty-seven Asiatics, all crowded together. Cadet Coleman was in command but he died during the following night and Cadet Clowe took over. During the first day they continued to lie to a sea anchor, keeping head to sea with the aid of oars on the lee side, and baling out constantly to keep down the level of water.

During the night of 5/6, the worst danger was from the large hatch-covers which were floating near the boat, collision with which would have shattered her bows. Mr Macrae, the third engineer, stationed himself in the bows and spent the night fending off the hatch-covers with a boat-hook. He never complained, but at dawn he was so exhausted that, quietly and peacefully, he lay down and died. His sacrifice buoyed up the remainder to further efforts.

The Asiatics felt the cold terribly, and were unable to help in the task of keeping the boat head to sea and in baling, so that the work fell on the British remaining. Several Asiatics and an army gunner also died during the night. Next day, 6 April, the sea anchor carried away and another was rigged. Everyone suffered from the bitter cold; their hands and feet became numbed and cramp of the stomach was endured by all. There was still a heavy sea, the boat started to fill up and the men sat with their feet in the icy water. There was a film of ice over everything, and their outer clothing was frozen stiff.

Faces, hands and feet were massaged with the oil provided, and Gunner Barnes, whose morale was high throughout this dreadful ordeal, was especially helpful in massaging those who had lost the energy to do it themselves.

Petty Officer Hadley, a naval gunner, was also outstanding, cheering people up, helping with distribution of rations and water, and taking the tiller later when a sail was raised.

On 7 April, Clowe cut his wrist and became delirious; and until he had recovered, Moore, supported and advised, as he generously writes, by Petty Officer Hadley, took charge of the boat.

By 8 April, there were only ten men left: nine British and one Asiatic, the seacunny, who remained cheerful and active until he died of cold the following day. Hadley and Barnes had made themselves the burial party and murmured a prayer over each body as it was dropped over the side. Only will power and prayer kept them going.

The weather then improved a little. An improvised sail was hoisted on an oar and the rowing was stopped; but the sea arose again during the night and the sail had to be taken down, and the sea anchor again used. That night the third radio officer and another gunner died of cold.

The situation then remained unchanged for three days. There was plenty of food to eat, but water had to be rationed, and hope was gradually fading.

Then at 1030 on 12 April, a Catalina flying-boat, of 84 Squadron (U.S.N.) operating from Iceland, was sighted; the boat fired red flares and the flying-boat circled and dropped a parcel, which however could not be reached owing to the rough sea.

Then the weather deteriorated further, the boat nearly capsized and a pair of oars was lost; hope which had been raised began to sink again. But at 1700, a Norwegian destroyer, the *St Albans* from the escort of convoy ON177, which already had rescued the survivors of the *Blitar*, hove in sight. It was too rough to transfer the men, but the destroyer made a lee and pumped oil on to the water; and within half an hour, the rescue ship *Zamalek* had arrived. She hoisted out the survivors in baskets, and soon all seven men were safe. The *Zamalek*'s skill and seamanship were outstanding.

Every care was lavished on the men, but only Clowe, French and Stevens retained all their limbs. Frostbite caused the amputation of both legs of Moore, Hadley and Theobald, and Barnes lost both feet.

They were transferred to hospital in Halifax on 21 April and thus ended an epic saga.

It is difficult to find words to express a proper admiration for the conduct of these men. Moore was only nineteen years of age. Clowe, not much older, had already survived the loss of the *Bhutan* by bombing and the *Trecarroll* by torpedo attack. Petty Officer Hadley was an elderly naval pensioner, but with the physical and mental courage of a much younger man.

Their courage and devotion, as well as the self-sacrifice of those who died, bring pride to the name of the British seaman.

# 11

# Random Thoughts on Convoy HX231

Once the euphoria of the group's return to harbour had worn off, there was much analysis of the results and much discussion of the reports of individual escorts.

It was as well for the peace of mind of all concerned that they had no conception whatever that while they talked, survivors of ships of the convoy were still tossing about the Atlantic in grim conditions, awaiting rescue.

The escort commander, probably wrongly, was slightly disappointed. A number of mistakes had been made which should have never occurred, and while the group had trained hard during the three months before the battle, it was evident that even more rigorous exercises were still needed.

There was much to do. Communication on convoy wave had to be improved. There must be no more failures to fire the correct number of depth-charges when attacking U-boats and the drill for the reloading of the depth-charges after they had been fired must be tightened.

The homing of the air escorts had not always worked as well as it should have done and further practice was needed; communication with aircraft also required improvement.

Most of all, the results of the short-range gunnery at night had been disappointing. It had been found extremely difficult to hit a submarine at very short range when the rate of change of bearing of the target was high; and the guns would be required to train very fast.

Paradoxically, our exercises had been carried out at too great a range, so a new type of exercise was designed. One of the members of the group towed a 'splash' target, representing a U-boat, at about 15 knots on a steady course. The firing ship steered to pass very close to the target on opposite courses at best speed, and as the name of the exercise, 'Pointblank', indicated, the range of firing was very short and the guns had to train fast to keep on their target.

Careful safety precautions were needed by day; at night the exercise became somewhat dangerous, and all sorts of measures had to be taken to prevent the towing ships from receiving some of the shots. However, it was a thoroughly realistic exercise which taught the guns' crews a great deal and helped to improve future performance.

There was a conference at the local tactical school at Derry, which was attended by the officers of B7 Group, by many of the aircrew which had escorted the convoy from 86 Squadron and by local staff officers.

The sequence of events during the convoy passage was discussed, the individual actions were analysed with the help of diagrams and as many lessons as possible were learnt for future benefit. It was a valuable conference, when officers from the ships and aircraft were able to explain what they had done and why. Differences of opinion were resolved one way or the other and future plans were worked out. In this quiet, informal atmosphere, it was possible for officers to put forward new ideas for consideration and some useful tactics emerged as a result.

In addition, the commanding officers met and went through the plans for the next convoy when the new ideas would be put into effect. The exercises which would be carried out before joining the next convoy were also discussed in detail so that every weakness which had been exposed would be put right. All that was wanted was some reasonable weather during the exercise period.

The new commanding officer of the *Loosestrife* had to be introduced to the group's plans and methods, and warned of the aspects of his ship's performance which needed improvement. Fortunately, he was an experienced and capable officer and was able to achieve much during the next spell of exercises. The *Loosestrife* was potentially a fine ship and good leadership soon produced the results which were to be shown in the coming convoy battle.

It was hoped that the group might visit Larne, where a Group Training Scheme had been established. A mock convoy, represented by the yacht *Philante*, was defended by one of the groups. Friendly submarines took the place of U-boats and Coastal Command and naval aircraft were able to practise their trade. It was a thoroughly practical affair and of great value.

At last, training in the Western Approaches Command was receiving the attention which it deserved. The situation was finally completed by the setting up of a joint Navy and Air Force anti-submarine school for airmen at the naval air station at Maydown, near Derry. Here the particular problems of aircraft working near convoys were discussed and exercised.

A great deal of thought was given to the U-boats and especially to the commanding officers. They had varied greatly in performance. Some had been bold and skilful, as had been shown by the successful attacks on ships in convoy; but others had been sensitive to harassment from the sea and the air.

It is now, after thirty years, possible to place oneself objectively in the position of a U-boat commander. The task of attacking a convoy at night on the surface must have been extremely alarming. Granted that the U-boat had a low silhouette and a high speed, yet it was not fitted with radar, and the enemy escorts with their special camouflage were difficult to see at night.

It must have been difficult to choose the gaps between the escorts through which to penetrate the screen, and once through, the risk of collision with merchant ships of the convoy was real. For although a diagram will show a convoy in a neat pattern with each ship in its station, in practice, especially at night, the pattern was most irregular and ships were seldom in exact station.

The days of men like Prien and Kretschmer, who used to remain in the middle of the convoy for long periods, steering convoy course and speed and picking off ships with deliberation from time to time, were over. Illumination by 'Snowflake' rocket had stopped such tactics, and once inside the convoy, the U-boat had now to fire its torpedoes and then escape through the columns as quickly as possible.

Given sufficient escorts, which HX231 did not have, and assuming that all the escorts had efficient centimetric radar, the night attack by U-boats on the surface must soon prove impossible.

As for day attacks by submerged submarines, these had proved possible in suitable conditions, as shown by the sinking of the *British Ardour*; but the attack which the *Tay* had frustrated showed that in good water conditions the asdic was effective.

It was clear that the submerged attack showed more promise in the future, and it seemed that the U-boats must acquire more speed with which to reach attacking positions, ahead of convoys.

A post-war analysis of the careers of the twenty commanding officers who were directed on to convoy HX231 shows what a short life the U-boat commander could expect in 1943 and 1944. Out of these twenty, two were sunk during the battle. Of the rest, only six survived the war and the remaining twelve lost their lives between 4 May 1943 and 31 July 1944. This is a loss rate unequalled by any other service and the manner in which U-boats continued to operate until the end is a tribute to the courage and morale of the crews, and of course of the commanding officers whose example was so important. One can only admire their endurance and bravery.

It is significant, I think, that the submarines which made bold attacks during HX231's passage, as opposed to those which attacked unescorted stragglers, were all lost during or shortly after the battle. Boldness was evidently bringing with it excessive risks.

After comparing the British and German records of the convoy, one conclusion seems to emerge which was not appreciated at the time. This was the need for many unpredictable movements and irregular zigzags by the escorts. Time and time again, one reads of U-boat attacks having been foiled by escorts who had no idea whatever that there was a submarine in the vicinity. Much 'to-ing and fro-ing', therefore, which seemed to be pointless at the time achieved an important purpose.

By now, the existence of the 'Milch Cow' U-boats was widely known on the Allied side and several officers wondered why it was not possible to search for them and to sink them at their mid-Atlantic rendezvous. It was not often realized, however, over what an enormous area the Atlantic extended and how difficult it would be to find one 'Milch Cow' in the vast expanse of ocean.

An attempt was made by American submarines – the *Hake* was the first – to find the fuelling U-boats in the spring of 1943, but there was no success. For obvious reasons, the project had to be very secret and news was released only after the war. Identification was a serious problem. The American submarines had to keep clear of Allied ships and aircraft and their operating areas were restricted. So it is hardly surprising that they never found a 'Milch Cow'.

It will have been noticed that the question of ramming a U-boat was mentioned frequently during the narrative; the *Tay* and others of the escort narrowly missed opportunities to ram which they would have taken if possible.

But the decision to ram or not was not as clear-cut as it first seemed. In the example of the destroyer escorting an aircraft carrier which was menaced by a surfaced submarine in a position to fire torpedoes, there could be no doubt. The destroyer rammed in order to save a valuable ship, irrespective of the damage to its own bow, which could be very great.

In the case of a slow escort which was part of a small group defending a large convoy, the situation was different. It might be wrong to ram, as the submarine might not sink, yet the escort's asdic would certainly be put out of action, if not worse damage suffered. Of course, if the battle were nearly over and no more attacks expected, then it might be right to ram.

But in the middle of the battle, the decision was more doubtful, and on balance it would seem best to avoid the ram and instead place a pattern of depth-charges as close as possible to the enemy.

One other consideration was important: the possibility of capturing a U-boat. To do so was the ambition of every escort group which each had its plans for such a *coup* – plans which were exercised with friendly submarines.

To try to capture or not depended on the situation. In the middle of a fierce battle with only a small escort present, it could not be attempted for the obvious reason that the ships could not be spared to tow and escort the quarry. But with a strong escort group, backed perhaps by a support group, the possibility of capture was always present, and was in fact achieved three times in the Atlantic during the war. The advantages were tremendous, and the yield of intelligence material likely to be very great. So if the object were to capture the U-boat, ramming must be avoided at all costs and a neatly placed pattern of depth-charges to frighten the submarine's crew would be used instead.

The question was often discussed at meetings of the captains of B7 Group, and it was agreed that to ram or not to ram depended upon the circumstances. But it was clear that there might be occasions when it would be right to refrain from ramming, which would require considerable moral courage on the part of the escort concerned.

As we have seen, one of the heart-rending features of convoy HX231 was the lack of a special rescue vessel to pick up survivors of sunken ships, a lack which caused the needless loss of so many lives.

The steadiness of the vast majority of the ships of the convoy had been impressive. They had been subject to terrifying experiences during two long nights, yet the station-keeping and discipline had been excellent. The ships which had wavered had paid with their lives.

During the period immediately after the convoy battle, the escorts had no firm news of three of the ships which had broken out or straggled. But there was no point in worrying over these tragedies. Worry would do the ships no good, and the important thing was to see that next time, no ship was sunk.

So inevitably a rather callous attitude was adopted which took the line that it was better to forget the past and concentrate on the future. It is only now, thirty years after, that one can cast aside the carapace of callousness, and appreciate more clearly the terrible experiences of the merchant seamen who were lost or who survived long journeys in boats.

Similarly, at the time, one took for granted the steadfastness of the ships in convoy, manned as they were by non-combatants of many nations. But today, with a clearer appreciation of what these men faced, day after day and year after year, one's admiration for their performance is very great indeed.

Finally, the outcome of the convoy battle had shown that B7 Group had an efficient staff, both of officers and men. A heavy load of work had been dealt with cheerfully and well; a mass of signals had been despatched or received without mistake, and the H/F D/F team had had a successful baptism of fire. No changes were needed here.

# 12

# Post-mortem on Convoy – Victory
# in the Atlantic

When looking back at the passage of convoy HX231 and trying to assess its results and its importance, it is convenient first to consult the German records which give a contemporary, if not always accurate, account of the battle. By combining German assessments with British judgements, it ought to be possible to produce an objective and informed survey.

The German U-boat headquarters War Diary contains the following summary of the operations against HX231:

> 'The operation against HX231 lasted from 4 to 7 April and extended over a distance of 700 miles. Twenty boats in all operated against the convoy, four of which probably failed to come up with it owing to shortage of fuel. The commanding officers of the boats were for the most part on their first operation.
>
> 'After the convoy was detected at midday on 4 April, it was anticipated that in view of the favourable position of the boats of Group *Löwenherz* all the boats would come up with the convoy during the first night.
>
> 'During the first day and night, eight boats contacted the convoy and, in spite of this, very little success was achieved during the first night. This was probably due primarily to the inexperience of the commanding officers. After the first attack during this night, part of the ships straggled from the convoy and it was possible to sink three.
>
> 'The convoy itself was reported, with breaks, until the evening of 6 April, but only by one or two boats. It was assumed that other boats were able to advance only with difficulty owing to the air defence becoming increasingly stronger. Numerous boats were bombed and some unable to carry out operations any further owing to damage sustained during evening of 7 April.

'The operation was then broken off since the boats were threatened by aircraft to an increasing degree in the vicinity of the coast.'

This is an accurate and straightforward account of the convoy, and I suspect must have been helped by information culled from the cryptographers. It gives no credit to the convoy escorts for their defence nor to the succession of attacks, all defeated, on the night of 5/6 April, but this is hardly surprising. Headquarters was anxious to attribute any lack of success to the inexperience of the commanding officers rather than to the ability of the defence, in order that confidence could be maintained as commanding officers gained their experience.

The War Diary's summary of statistical results is less accurate:

'In all eight ships, consisting of 58,000 tons, were sunk, and of these five came from the convoy. Also one escort was sunk. A further three ships were torpedoed. Two boats were probably lost in the operations agains this convoy, *U632* and *U635*. A further five boats were heavily damaged by bombs or depth-charges.'

The claim of ships sunk and torpedoed is rather greater than the facts merited and the mysterious sunk escort appears again! The most significant aspect of the whole entry is the emphasis on the inexperience of the commanding officers, and another contemporary report from the German headquarters reads:

'Most of the boats were on their first operation, which explained why the eight U-boats achieved so little in the all-important first-night surprise.'

Here again, we have more evidence that the Germans did not realize the extent to which surprise was lost, in fact, owing to the radio signals of the pack and to the good work of the solitary H/F D/F fitted ship in the escort.

This account went on to say:

'A rearrangement of U-boats followed the end of this engagement resulting in two new groups, each of ten boats, being stationed on each side of the air gap and another of seven boats farther to the south in case the shipping route should be switched to lower latitudes.'

This paragraph is interesting as it shows that the Germans used the same wording to describe the 'air gap', and also because by the formation of three new groups, there is clear indication of their intention to prosecute the battle with even more vigour.

There is one final extract of interest, which comes from the official German history compiled soon after the war, when some additional records were available. It runs.

> '*The last partially successful attacks on convoys.*
>
> 'After the operation against HX230, only one tanker, *U463*, was available to refuel sixteen boats due to return to base. This left only a single Group *Löwenherz* available for operations, so on 3 April, its boats proceeded westward from a position 400 miles south-eastwards of Cape Farewell, making contact the following day with convoy HX231.
>
> 'The initial position was favourable, the weather was suitable for the pursuit until 7 April, but it resulted in the sinking of only six ships with damage claimed to one escort and three more ships.
>
> 'In this case, U-boat numbers were adequate, the relatively small results being ascribed to difficulty in attaining attacking positions owing to the presence of carrier-borne aircraft.'

The heading of the paragraph is interesting, indicating as it does the opinion that the sinking of six ships (including stragglers) was a 'partial success'. It is also interesting to see that the emphasis on the inexperience of the commanding officers has been omitted in this post-war judgement. The only fault in what is otherwise a fair and reasonably accurate account of the engagement is the extraordinary mention of carrier-borne aircraft, none of which, of course, were ever in company with the convoy.

When we come to consider contemporary British records, it is plain from the escort commander's report that he was pleased, on balance, with the end result, which he had feared at several stages of the passage might be a good deal worse.

I think that it is worth quoting from his last few paragraphs:

'9. Air cover again showed itself to be the key to the problem. The work of the Liberators on 5, 6 and 7 April cannot be too highly praised. They were quick to appreciate the requirements and effective in their execution.

'10. I was pleased to have topped up *Vidette, Pink* and *Tay* before the battle commenced. *Vidette* and *Pink* would not otherwise have lasted the course. It should be unnecessary to stress the importance of constant practice in refuelling at sea, even when a top-up is not strictly necessary. Good drill cuts the time down enormously and with it fuelling is possible in almost any weather.

'11. The experiences of *Vaarlangen, Blitar* and *Sunoil* should again bring home to masters the danger of either breaking out of convoy or of straggling.

'12. I was surprised that U-boats continued to keep contact during the low visibility of the night of 6/7 April, the day of 7 April and the night of 7/8, despite evasive turns by the convoy. I can only conclude that they achieved this by listening on hydrophones or else by radar. It is very unlikely that any sighted the convoy.

'13. I had been looking forward with some alarm to the prospect of directing the activities of a senior officer in the support group. In the event, the situation was easy to control due to the ready co-operation of E.G.4 and his ships. There is no doubt in my own mind that it is essential for the senior officer of the close screen to be in general charge.

'In connection with the tactics of support groups, I would like to state that I consider it essential for at least eight ships fitted with Type 271 radar to remain on the close screen at night.

'14. "Snowflake" illumination of the convoy was reasonably effective when it started, but in both cases it was too late. Once started it was easily controlled by W/T. I am still convinced that illumination by "Snowflake" immediately after a torpedoing is the only means of detecting the submarine responsible and suggest that it is essential that the importance and value of the immediate illumination by "Snowflake" should again be impressed on masters.

'15. The commodore handled the convoy with ability and was easy to work with – I am most grateful for his help.

with the exception of the ships which broke convoy, the station-keeping was good.

'16. All escorts worked hard and well as a team. I feel that the loss of three ships among a heavy concentration of U-boats was comparatively light and due to their efforts.'

There is little to add to these comments, which were made the day after the return to harbour and represented the impressions which lay most heavily on the escort commander's mind. They are full of detail, perhaps too much so, but after such an ordeal, it is often the irritating, small points which take an excessive importance in the mind. But, detail apart, the importance of air escort was very fully appreciated.

The senior officer at Londonderry, Commodore Simpson, made several remarks in his forwarding report on the action, but does not seem to have summed up the results as a whole. It is however pleasing to read one paragraph:

> 'The senior officer, escort, appears to have used the very satisfactory air cover to the utmost advantage particularly without any waste of patrol time. Homing was good, particularly on 7 April, when weather conditions were poor.'

Finally, it can be recorded that the convoy received a mention at a meeting of the Cabinet Committee on anti-U-boat warfare in London on 7 April, before the battle was finally concluded. Admiral Horton is reported in the minutes as having said:

> 'In spite of repeated attacks between 30 March [sic] and 6 April, the convoy lost only three ships (three stragglers – fate unknown). This was a good example of the results which could be achieved by an efficient escort commander and a fairly good trained group which had been given splendid air support.'

I do not wish to claim anything exceptional for convoy HX231. Other convoys endured heavier losses and other convoys were attacked in greater strength. It was, however, typical of a large-scale convoy operation which lasted several days, and for this reason, as I have earlier suggested, worth detailed analysis.

Of the convoys which came later, HX232 lost three ships, HX233 lost one ship and HX234 had one ship torpedoed which did not sink. Perhaps the easiest way to sum up the passage of convoy HX231 is to say that it represented the 'beginning of the end'.

And now we turn to a summary of how the 'end', which convoy HX231 had begun, was finally achieved in the short space of only eight weeks: eight weeks in which despair was replaced by confidence and looming defeat by conceded victory.

In the first week of April 1943, Admiral Edelsten, who was in charge of Trade and of anti-U-boat operations at the Admiralty, wrote:

> 'Up to 20 March, there seemed a real danger that the enemy would achieve his aim of severing the routes which united Great Britain and the North American continent; after that date, his strength seemed to ebb.'

HX231 seemed to start this ebb and the convoys which followed continued the good work. At U-boat headquarters, there was apparently still no indication that the writing on the wall had been observed. Packs were being formed, convoys were being attacked and the commanding officers were being urged to throw themselves at the enemy.

Edelsten's staff report written at the end of April says:

> 'Apparently over half the enemy's Atlantic force operated during April in the North-West Atlantic and there appeared to be a tendency to give a *wider offing* to British air bases as opposed to Canadian, thus producing a centre of gravity to the area west of 35° west. Probably the main scheme of patrols for the interruption of trans-atlantic convoys is to form up several groups of some ten to twelve U-boats on or near on an arc of 600 miles radius from Newfoundland in the sector between 070° and 130° from St John's, Newfoundland. Pack tactics are still being used and the size tending to grow; probably over twenty U-boats not infrequently make contact with a convoy. The areas south and south-east of Cape Farewell have been and will remain highly dangerous.'

This statement seems to have been remarkably accurate and fore-seeing and shows how well the Admiralty appreciated the situation. The report went on to say that U-boat activity was largely confined to the North Atlantic which Dönitz still believed would provide, in the 'air gap', the 'soft spot' which he was always seeking to probe. There was no activity off the North and South American coasts and only a few attacks in the West Indies area.

In addition to HX231, concentrations of U-boats had made contact with several convoys, and four, bound for the United Kingdom, had suffered casualties, which were however comparatively light compared to those in March.

In the first week in May, the same staff report made these cogent remarks:

> 'Historians of this war are likely to single out the months of April and May 1943, as the *critical period* during which strength began to ebb away from the German U-boat offensive – not because of lower figures of shipping or higher numbers of U-boats sunk, but because for the first time, U-boats failed to press home their attacks on convoys when favourably situated to do so.
>
> 'The numbers of U-boats operating was as great at the end of April as it ever has been; U-boat construction still overtops casualties, and, despite the increasing effort of our air and surface attacks, the U-boat fleet continues to grow in numbers, though more slowly than before. Yet its effective strength appears to be waning.'

If these remarks had been shown to one of the escorts of convoy ONS5 which was then *en route* for Canada, the language would have been unprintable, but other than the fact that he seems to be about a fortnight too early in his estimates, the writer of the report was extremely accurate.

By now, Dönitz and his staff must have had an inkling of what was in store, for he is quoted as having said at the end of April, 'Who ever thinks offensive operations against convoys are no longer possible is a weakling.' Within three weeks, he was confessing to have joined the band of weaklings himself!

At the start of May, however, the actual situation, as opposed to staff officers' estimates of what would happen, was that there were 116 U-boats in the North Atlantic and that a dramatic German offensive was planned. On the British side, the five support groups were settling down to their task and three had been joined by an escort carrier which brought a formidable increase in strength. These American-built, mass-produced ships carried a good complement of specially designed anti-submarine aircraft as well as a few fighters for use when in range of the German Focke-Wolf Condors which were to be met with the convoys to Gibraltar and West Africa.

All was poised for a continuation of the battle therefore, and May accordingly opened with a bloody and long drawn out clash between several packs of submarines and convoy ONS5.

ONS5 was a very slow convoy. Most of the ships were elderly and had difficulty in keeping up, and being light in ballast was a grave disadvantage in the constant gales which beset them throughout the passage.

There were forty-two ships in all, escorted by B7 Group, fresh from convoy HX231. The group had been strengthened by the inclusion of the destroyer *Duncan*, the ship of the escort commander, and by the attachment of two rescue trawlers to pick up survivors. The corvette *Sunflower* had taken the place of the *Alisma*, which had gone to refit. There were only two tankers for refuelling escorts, and one of them was soon to prove that its gear was useless, being fitted with canvas instead of rubber hosepipe. However, the usual refuelling exercises were carried on during the first two days after meeting the convoy off Oversay in the North Channel on 22 April.

These first two days were uneventful except for the weather which gradually worsened until a gale was blowing which eventually caused two of the ships to collide. One had to be sent back to Iceland for repairs, but no escort could be spared to look after her.

There was a scare on 24 April when the Admiralty announced that a U-boat had gained contact with the convoy. Everyone was alerted and the *Duncan* tried to top up with fuel oil from the

*British Lady*. Unfortunately the weather was too bad and the hose parted.

That evening to the relief of all, the Admiralty signalled that it had been a false alarm and that the convoy was still unreported. Moreover that afternoon a Flying Fortress of 206 Squadron had attacked and sunk *U710*, which was lying on the track ahead. Perhaps the convoy might pass through the patrol line without being sighted?

On 27 April, the weather improved a little, and the *Duncan* and the *Vidette* were able to refuel. Oil consumption had exercised the escort commander's mind so much that he had planned to go to Greenland to top up if the weather had not relented.

On the next day, 28 April, a U-boat was heard transmitting from dead ahead of the convoy, and as the signal was loud and close, it was certain that the convoy had been reported. In fact, it was *U650* which shadowed all day. Fourteen other U-boats were ordered to join in and attack that same night and it was evident to the escorts that there was another long battle ahead. That sinking feeling was again felt!

Due to bad weather at base, no aircraft had been available to escort the convoy and stop the pack assembling, though there were some patrols flown in the vicinity which disturbed the U-boats' movements a little.

The escorts carried out several sweeps down H/F D/F bearings during the afternoon, but none resulted in a sighting until 1830 when the *Duncan* and the *Tay* together saw a submarine. But no asdic contact was obtained and after some depth-charges had been dropped as a discouragement, they had to return to the convoy, so as to be in station before dark.

Placing the field was easy. There was a strong wind and sea from the port quarter, so that the starboard bow was left unprotected and the main strength concentrated to port with the *Duncan* on the port quarter. The placing had been right. The first attack was dealt with by the *Sunflower* on the port bow; then followed no less than four attacks from the port quarter, all of which were driven off by the *Duncan*. Finally, an attack was defeated by the *Snowflake* on the port beam. It had been a busy night with no losses to the convoy and two U-boats had been damaged.

At dawn, sweeps were carried out astern and ahead of the convoy without success. Then three hours later, when the escort was beginning to congratulate itself on a successful start to the battle, the *U258* penetrated the screen from ahead and sank the second ship in the fourth column. It had been a bold attack, and although some contacts were attacked in the subsequent search, *U258* got away unscathed.

On 30 April, there was much signal activity near the convoy and again some contacts attacked without success. The weather was getting worse again and was hindering both escorts and U-boats. That night the destroyer *Oribi*, the first of the promised Third Support Group, arrived and took her place on the screen. The night was quiet and the U-boats were evidently prevented by the weather from attacking.

The day of 30 April was also quiet except for the weather which was causing the convoy to scatter slowly all over the ocean. The following night was disturbed only by one sighting of a U-boat which was attacked without result. By now, the gale had forced most of the U-boats to dive and they were losing all touch with the convoy. On the morning of 2 May, Dönitz called off the pack which was ordered to reform astern.

The convoy was now badly scattered and Liberators from 120 Squadron flew great distances to help shepherd the ships back to the commodore's fold. By the end of the day, some thirty-two ships were in the main body, while the *Pink* was looking after a small team of four ships some miles away.

That evening, the rest of the Third Support Group commanded by Captain McCoy joined, bringing the total to five destroyers, and took their stations on the outer screen. The weather was still very bad, refuelling was impossible, and at dusk, the *Duncan* proceeded to St John's, Newfoundland, arriving later with almost empty tanks, and leaving the convoy to be commanded by Lieutenant-Commander Sherwood in the *Tay*. The *Duncan* was soon followed by three of the support group's destroyers.

On the German side, Dönitz had on 3 May formed a new and

large Group (*Fink*), which he told to intercept convoy SC128 whose position was known. SC128 passed through the patrol line without being sighted but unfortunately, ONS5 blundered, to the surprise of both sides, into the middle of the line on 4 May.

Dönitz recorded:

> 'The initial positions for a convoy battle had never been more favourable. Thirty boats of Group *Fink* were in the patrol line, with only eight miles between each boat, and the convoy was sighted right in the middle of this line. Moreover, eleven boats of Group *Amsel* were ahead of the convoy.'

In addition, the shocking flying conditions and the distance from base made close air escort impossible, so that aircraft were unable to play their part in the battle which was confined to escorts and U-boats and proved to be as bitter as any in the whole war. However, a Canso aircraft of the R.C.A.F. which was unable to reach the convoy, sank *U630* which was lying in wait well ahead and so cut down the numbers of the attackers.

There was much signal activity round the convoy throughout the day of 4 May, and some submarines were seen and put down. It was certain that a big battle was building up.

The struggle that night was intense. Six merchant ships were sent to the bottom by U-boats which pressed their home attacks right into the convoy. The escorts were very busy and had driven off several more attempts. The rescue trawlers had been engaged all night in picking up survivors and had proved worth their weight in gold.

At daylight on 5 May, there were two ships of the support group, and one destroyer, one frigate and three corvettes of the close escort present, and the weather eased and allowed some badly needed refuelling. But during that day, four more ships were lost to attacks pressed home by U-boats which dived under the convoy. The situation was very grave as only one attack had been made on a submarine, and that by the *Oribi*, some distance away from the convoy. No air cover was available.

Some miles astern, the captain of the *Pink* was having an excit-

ing time with his small convoy. He sank the *U192* after a determined hunt, but lost one merchant ship.

By dusk, the air was filled with U-boat signalling. German
reports state that the perimeter of the convoy was crowded with
U-boats waiting their turn to attack. The only news to relieve the
gloom was that of the arrival of the First Support Group from
St John's in a day or two. In the words of Captain McCoy of the
*Offa*, 'the convoy faced annihilation'.

Dönitz, who understood the situation and realized that the
convoy would soon be under air cover from Newfoundland,
signalled the boats to make one more tremendous effort, using
'utmost energy'. He also ordered them to fight back on the surface
if aircraft did appear.

On that night of 5/6 May, fifteen U-boats tried to attack
ONS5. But providence provided a fog which hampered the submarines while allowing the escorts to surprise them by using their
radar. The performance of the escorts was superb; the determination of the U-boats was striking. During the night, no less than
twenty-five attacks were driven off, four U-boats were sunk and
several damaged and not one ship of the convoy was touched.

It had been a great victory for the defence, and at 0915 next
morning, Dönitz called off Group *Fink* and the eight-day battle
was ended. The final score was a loss of twelve ships from the
convoy, against which could be set heavy submarine sinkings.
Aircraft patrolling near the convoy had sunk two, one was sunk
by the First Support Group *en route* to the convoy, and five were
sunk by the close escort and the Third Support Group. In addition
two U-boats collided with each other on 3 May and both perished.
The Germans had lost ten U-boats altogether.

Perhaps the outstanding feature of this display of skill and
courage by the escorts was that it had been achieved despite a
minimum of air escort. Sherwood and his ships should be very
proud of what they had done.

Two more convoys, HX237 and SC129, were at sea in mid-May.
HX237 which was escorted by C2 Group, was supported by the
escort carried *Biter* and the Fifth Support Group. Its position was

obtained from deciphered signals, together with that of SC129, and a total of thirty-six submarines was ordered to attack the two convoys.

HX237 lost three stragglers, but *U89* was sunk by aircraft from the *Biter* and escorts and *U456* by Coastal Command aircraft and escorts. Co-operation between aircraft and escorts was excellent. No ship in convoy was lost, though a Swordfish aircraft from the *Biter* was shot down by a U-boat. Aircraft from the escort carrier had closed the 'air gap'.

Convoy SC129 was escorted by B2 Group and later received support from the *Biter* and her ships. This convoy, which was also covered by Liberators from 86 Squadron, lost three ships; but the escort commander's ship, the *Hesperus*, sank *U186* and a Liberator, dropping the newly produced homing torpedo, sank *U266*.

A total of thirty-six submarines had failed to dispatch more than five ships from the two convoys and had lost four of their number in the process. Now at last there were clear signs that attacks were being pressed home with less determination.

It was the same story with convoy ON184, escorted by C1 Group and supported by the American Sixth Support Group, which contained the escort carrier *Bogue*; and with convoy HX239, escorted by B3 Group and supported by the escort carrier *Archer* and the Fourth Support Group. No ships were lost from the convoys; an Avenger aircraft from the *Bogue* sank *U657* and a Swordfish from the *Archer*, using the new A/S rocket, despatched *U752*.

Finally came convoy SC130, escorted by our old friend B7 Group which had only just time to recover from the effects of the battle round ONS5. This slow convoy was assailed by a pack of nineteen boats, but by a combination of circumstances which included constant air cover by day, the help of the First Support Group, and the discipline of the convoy which executed numerous emergency turns with the precision of a battle fleet, all attacks were beaten off, and not one single ship was lost.

Moreover the *Duncan* and the *Snowflake* shared the credit for *U381*, the Support Group sank *U209*, aircraft from 120 Squadron dispatched *U954* and *U258* when providing close escort, while

Hudsons on patrol near the convoy accounted for *U646* and *U273*.

Dönitz had lost six U-boats and their success had been nil. The failure was too much to bear, and in his own words:

> 'The overwhelming superiority achieved by the enemy defence was finally proved beyond dispute in the operations against convoys SC130 and HX239. The convoy escorts worked in exemplary harmony with the specially trained support groups. To that must be added the continuous air cover which was provided by the carrier-borne (for HX239) and long-range aircraft, most of them equipped with the new radar. . . . Operations could only be resumed if we succeeded in radically increasing the fighting power of the U-boats.
>
> 'This was the logical conclusion to which I came, and accordingly I withdrew the boats from the north Atlantic. On 24 May, I ordered them to proceed, using the utmost caution, to the area south-west of the Azores. We had lost the Battle of the Atlantic.'

It was not long before Admiral Horton appreciated the situation. On 26 May, he sent the following signal to his command:

> 'The Battle of the Atlantic has taken a definite turn in our favour during the past two months, and the returns show an ever-increasing toll of U-boats and decreasing losses of merchant ships in convoy.
>
> 'All escort groups, support groups, escort carriers and their aircraft, and aircraft of the various air commands, have contributed to this great achievement, which is the outcome of hard work, hard training and determination on the part of all officers and men of the surface forces and air units involved. Quite apart from the spectacular kills which have been achieved by the escort groups and support groups, many notable victories have been achieved by the safe and timely arrival of a number of convoys in the face of heavy enemy attack.
>
> 'Outstanding among the results is the performance of B7 Group (Commander Gretton) despite the enforced absence

of their leader,★ aided by the 3rd and 1st Support Groups (Captain McCoy and Commander Brewer respectively) while escorting and covering ONS5 which resulted in such wholesale destruction of the enemy; the successful passage of HX237 escorted by C2 Group (Commander Chavasse) and that of SC129 escorted by B2 Group (Commander McIntyre) both being supported by *Biter* and 5th Support Group; also of HX234 escorted by B4 Group (Commander Day) and supported by the 4th Support Group (Captain Scott Moncrieff).

'More recently comes the heavy defeat of the enemy during the passage of SC130, escorted and supported by B7 Group and the 1st Support Group, and HX239, escorted and supported by B3 Group (Commander Evans) and *Archer* and the 4th Support Group, which resulted in the enemy quickly giving up the battle.

'Particularly gratifying is the outstanding success of the aircraft of the escort carriers *Bogue, Biter* and *Archer*, who have given invaluable service in the battle. We owe much also to the help of the Home Fleet destroyers who came to our aid and acquitted themselves so brilliantly in this unaccustomed type of warfare. Much sterling work has also been done by the escorts on the Gibraltar to Freetown runs.

'The tide of battle has checked if not turned and the enemy is showing signs of strain in the face of heavy attacks by our sea and air forces. Now is the time to strike and strike hard, bearing in mind always that the secret of success is trained efficiency and immediate readiness for every conceivable emergency.'

In the summer of 1943, Dönitz, after removing his U-boats from the North Atlantic, tried to find 'soft spots' where the defence was weak. In June, he decided to attack in the Central Atlantic area through which convoys were bound from America to the Mediterranean, where vast quantities of supplies were needed for the invasions of Sicily and Italy. Shore-based air cover was non-existent due to lack of bases on the convoy route.

★ The *Duncan* had been forced to leave the convoy because of fuel shortage just before the climax of the battle.

However, the American escort carriers (C.V.E.s) came into their own and had many successes, notably against U-boats attacking convoy GUS7A which was bound for Gibraltar from the United States.

They imposed a severe defeat on Group *Trautz* of seventeen boats, and steered the convoy unscathed past the patrol line, while killing one U-boat. In the two months which followed, the carriers had it all their own way and despatched fifteen U-boats in the area around the Azores, forcing the Germans to evacuate the Central as well as the North Atlantic.

During this summer too the Bay of Biscay offensive by aircraft of Coastal Command working from the south-west of England had its most successful period, due mainly to tactical errors by the German High Command. Many boats were being sunk in transit, and the outlook for the U-boat arm was grim.

In October 1943, a new, brief offensive was launched in the North Atlantic, loudly heralded in German propaganda. The U-boats, fitted with a new weapon, the homing torpedo GNAT, gained some temporary success but were quickly defeated by the combined efforts of the scientists and by the surface and air escorts.

After this, activity was low until the arrival in service of the *Schnorchel* breathing-tube in 1944, which allowed the U-boats to use their diesel engines while dived, and so avoid detection by radar when charging their batteries on the surface. Operations were now possible in coastal waters, and the conflict moved from the ocean nearer inshore.

An especially intense effort was put into an attempt to interfere with operation 'Overlord', the invasion of Europe, in June 1944. But Coastal Command 'flooded' the approaches to the English Channel with patrolling aircraft, while a large number of A/S ships were employed as escorts to the invasion convoys or as support groups in the approaches to the Channel. The German attack was beaten off with few casualties to Allied shipping and with many sinkings of U-boats, especially those which were not fitted with the *Schnorchel*.

So, while a very considerable effort, both surface and air, was needed continually to deal with the German submarine and no let-up was ever possible, the enemy, which continued to operate until the last day of the war, was never able to cause the same degree of anxiety nor was there ever again any real doubt as to the ultimate result.

It is fair, therefore, to conclude that May 1943 did indeed see the main victory in the Battle of the Atlantic.

# 13

# Why did the Germans Lose the Battle of the Atlantic in the Spring of 1943?

It is a fascinating exercise to try to decide on the reasons for the dramatic reversal of fortune in the Battle of the Atlantic in April 1943. There can be no doubt that in March the situation was extremely serious. The losses of shipping had been appallingly high, there appeared to be only two months' reserves of food and materials left in the country at the prevailing loss rate and the Admiralty was very pessimistic on the outcome.

Yet on 22 May Dönitz conceded defeat in the battle and withdrew his U-boats from the northern sector of the Atlantic, leaving only one or two weather reporters to send him meteorological information. After the carnage of March, and the losses of April and May, not one merchant ship was sunk in the Atlantic north of 31° N, during June.

Why did this happen? It was, of course, due to a number of circumstances and cannot be attributed to one in particular or even to one or two in combination. Some of the reasons were of long standing and some arose at the time of crisis.

With some trepidation, therefore, I will discuss these many factors and try to draw some broad conclusions on their relative merits. It is a difficult and delicate task, and I will not attempt to be dogmatic; nevertheless, some of the conclusions may be controversial and I hope that they will be found interesting.

After all, a change from a situation in which 'defeat faced them [the Allies] in the face' to one in which Dönitz gave up the battle only two months later, must have been as startling and speedy a reversal of fortune as any in the long history of warfare.

I must apologize for some inevitable repetition which is necessary if a fair picture is to be given.

·     ·     ·     ·     ·

I consider first the men concerned on both sides of the battle, for ultimately they must provide a most important factor in any aspect. To quote Roskill (Vol. II, p. 355): 'It was a battle between *men*, aided certainly by all the instruments and devices which science could provide, but still one which would be decided by the skill and endurance of men, and by the intensity of the moral purpose which inspired them.'

Thirty years have passed since the peak of the struggle was reached and it should be possible to stand back from the distorted propaganda-ridden attitudes of the times, when the enemy were always evil men inspired by wrong-doers, and to adopt a dispassionate approach.

In British propaganda, the German U-boat arm was portrayed as entirely Nazi-dominated and the crews as pirates without a redeeming virtue. The occasions, and they were by no means rare, when the U-boats put themselves at risk by helping survivors of ships which they had sunk were ignored.

In fact the German Navy was far less Nazi-dominated than either of the other two services, and the men in the U-boat arm were brave and tough, mostly volunteers, and all determined to serve their country with a high sense of duty.

Their morale, naturally, wavered from time to time, depending on the progress of the war at sea, but it never fell to a low level and was usually very high. Certainly the U-boat crews endured long cruises under conditions of great danger and discomfort and always seemed ready to continue despite periods of very heavy losses.

Indeed, there must have been few services in the world which would lose 32,000 out of 39,000 officers and men, yet at a time of overwhelming defeat retain their cohesion and discipline. I can speak from personal knowledge as I visited the Flensburg and Bergen U-boat bases in May 1945 and saw from careful inspection the state of the remaining U-boats and the morale of their crews.

On the British side the greatest attribute was confidence. The men at sea, as opposed to some of the desk warriors, could just not imagine defeat. Britain always won her maritime wars, and even at the worst times there was a complete determination that this one would be won too.

The ships of the Western Approaches Command were manned mainly by wartime sailors who learnt their trade remarkably quickly, and the saying that an island race breeds good sailors cannot be wrong. But it should not be forgotten what a great part the Royal Canadian Navy took in the Atlantic Battle. This navy expanded in a fantastic manner, starting with only a handful of ships and ending with many hundreds. Some growing pains were naturally suffered in the process, but especially in the last three years of the war, the Canadians carried a burden equal to that of the Royal Navy in the work of convoy protection, and performed admirably. Escorts manned by other countries like Norway, Holland, Poland, Free France, Belgium and of course, the United States, also took part; but their contribution while significant could not compare with that of the Royal Navy and the Royal Canadian Navy.

The officers and men of the Royal Air Force and of the Royal Canadian Air Force also performed with valour and determination Co-operation was far better than that between the Germany Navy and Air Force, which never succeeded in working amicably together. The reader will notice that there is no mention of the German Air Force in the account of convoy HX231, because this was routed too far to the north for the German Air Force to be able to reach the scene. Nevertheless, in the operations around the convoys to Gibraltar and to West Africa, which were in range of the German aircraft, the Luftwaffe's attempts to help the U-boats were singularly unsuccessful.

But in comparing the relative merits of the combatants on both sides now that passion has cooled, I think that it would be wrong to say that either side had a monopoly of skill or courage, and that in assessing the reasons for the Allied victory, the ability and morale of the men concerned did not sway the issue one way or the other.

When one considers technical subjects, it is not easy to make a comparisons between the U-boats on the one hand and the ships and escorts on the other.

There can be no doubt that the U-boats were very well designed and built, and one shudders at the thought of what would have happened if Germany had started the war with the 300 submarines which Dönitz demanded, instead of the handful – less than twenty-five ocean-going boats – which he got.

The Type VII, which formed the majority of the fleet, was ideal for the job. It was quick-diving, easily manœuvrable and tough. The Type IX, which was larger, with a longer endurance, suffered from its size and was slow to dive and difficult to manœuvre. The large 'Milch Cow' fuel tankers were successful and well designed.

All the boats were very reliable and were intended to operate in the weather of the North Atlantic. In 1938 and 1939, Dönitz had held large-scale exercises against convoys in the Bay of Biscay, where the weather can be very rough, and many lessons had been learnt which led to modifications of the designs. The engines were reliable, the instruments excellent, and Dönitz must have been well pleased with the results of all his planning before the war.

Typically, the British carried out little or no planning before the war and started with far too few ships and aircraft to defend a convoy system, while the ships and aircraft available were unsuitable for the task, and designed for different roles.

Taking the ships first, the main brunt of the work first fell on the 'S', 'V' and 'W' class destroyers of the First World War which had been built for quick dashes into the North Sea with the Grand Fleet and did not have enough endurance for convoy passages across the Atlantic. As a result, until refuelling at sea was instituted as a regular feature of convoy work, and until some of the destroyers had been modified to increase their endurance, it was not possible to give convoys protection right across the ocean, and many losses occurred from U-boats after the convoys had dispersed or before their escorts had joined for the eastern passage.

The other mainstay of the convoy escort force, the corvette, was hurriedly produced in large numbers at the beginning of the war from a trawler design. The corvette had many excellent features and without it the convoy system would have collapsed, but it was too slow and could not overtake a U-boat at full speed on the surface, which was a grave disadvantage especially in night actions. Only when frigates like the *Tay*, and later classes with greater speed, were built, did things get better.

As to the equipment fitted, it too seemed always to have been designed for short cruises rather than for the prolonged gales of the Atlantic (and Arctic). The stern fact that much of the equipment was immersed in salt spray or water for long periods took some time to be appreciated by the designers, and initially it did not stand up to the hard treatment it received.

One of the virtues of the British escorts, however, was the reliability of the propulsion machinery. The destroyers had well-proven engines which had run well, in some cases for twenty-five years. They were old-fashioned but they never broke down. As to the frigates and corvettes, they were fitted with simple and well-tried reciprocating engines and little trouble was experienced.

In general, however, the British started the war inadequately prepared with too few escorts which, in turn, were unsuited to the task. It was not until the summer of 1943 that enough new ships and new weapons started to emerge from the shipyards.

In the air, the situation was even worse. At the start of the war convoy protection came low in the list of priorities, and as a result the few aircraft provided for the Command were unsuitable for A/S warfare, and their crews were not well trained in the task.

Gradually and slowly things got better. New types of aircraft were introduced or, more usually, heavy bombers were converted to the new role; the training of aircrews improved; and most important of all, the anti-submarine task generally was recognized as first priority. But it took three years of war and much sterile and useless argument before this improved situation was reached.

It is fruitless to try to allocate blame for this shocking state of affairs. Both the Admiralty and the Air Ministry were at fault, and the British Governments of the thirties with their delayed approach to taking measures to oppose the menace of Hitler must also be held responsible.

We must return to our original question, however, from this

wide digression, and declare that, on balance, the German U-boat was in the spring of 1943 more suitable for its task than the average Allied escort, surface or air.

When it comes to the equipment fitted in the ships and aircraft, however, the situation seems to me to be quite different; and the British held a definite advantage. I divide the general term 'equipment' into two parts: the first, hardware such as weapons; and the second, electronic devices which will include the use of asdic, radar and H/F D/F.

Before discussing the details, it might be interesting to consider why this happened, for the Germans are unrivalled in the world in technical prowess, and during the war, they led in many fields such as the V1 and V2 rockets. I believe that the British made better use of their scientists. For one thing, the scientists were able to understand what they were trying to achieve and scientist/naval officer teams tackled each particular problem together, whereas German scientists were kept isolated and told to get on to some project, the use of which they did not entirely comprehend.

With apologies to Roskill and to the author, who was a member of the Anti-Submarine Division of the Naval Staff at the Admiralty, I quote some doggerel which seems to express admirably what I am trying to say:

> 'Gaily the backroom boys
> Peddling their gruesome toys,
> Come in and make a noise,
> Oozing with science.
> Humbly their aid we've sought;
> Without them we're as nought,
> For modern wars are fought
> By such alliance.'

Secondly, and probably even more importantly, the British had scientists in the operation rooms ashore, both naval and air force, where by the use of statistical method and by their scientific approach to problems, they were able to suggest new ideas and improvements both in the field of tactics and even of strategy. These operational research sections were as much a part of the operational team as the professional naval and air force officers with whom they worked.

We have already seen how Professor Blackett managed to persuade a reluctant Naval Staff to increase the size of convoys in a way which allowed the strength of the escorts to be increased at little inconvenience. One other example might help to make the point.

One day Blackett was watching the map of the Atlantic at the combined headquarters of the Western Approaches Command and of 15 Group, R.A.F. at Derby House, Liverpool. On the map were shown the position of the German U-boats as known by the Admiralty, and also the tracks of the aircraft patrols which were flying in the Western Approaches area. Blackett worked out on the back of an envelope the number of U-boats which should have been sighted by these aircraft, given a reasonable look-out by both sides. He then found out the number of U-boats which had been actually sighted and discovered that it was considerably less than should have been expected.

The first question he asked was, 'What colour are the aircraft painted?' and was told 'black', because they were mostly bombers which had been working in Bomber Command. He immediately suggested that the aircraft be painted white, so that they should be more difficult to see against a cloud background. Trials were carried out and this was done. The number of sightings increased at once and it was plain that previously the submarines had been diving before they could be sighted, because the black aircraft were so easy to see. There are many other examples of the use of operational research in the Battle of the Atlantic. The Germans did not introduce scientists into the U-boat headquarters until the end of 1943 when a team brought in at once produced some new and ingenious ideas. But it was too late.

With the actual production of new technical hardware by the spring of 1943, to which I now return, there seems to be little in it. The British introduced the 'Hedgehog' anti-submarine weapon, and some much improved explosives for depth-charges, both for ships and for aircraft; the American homing torpedo and the

British air-delivered rocket were just coming into service. The Germans produced the pattern-running torpedo which had a good chance of hitting a target when fired at a convoy, but their torpedoes were not reliable and had an inherent fault in the depth-keeping mechanism which was not put right until well on into the war. The main German advances, such as the *Schorchel* and the GNAT, a homing torpedo which listened for the propellors of an escort, homed on to them and then blew the stern off, did not come into service until late in 1943 when the main battle had been won.

In one other respect the Germans were well ahead but, due to policy changes, damage by Allied bombing and lack of support from Hitler, the project came into fruition only during the last few days of the war.

I refer to two new types of submarine: the first as exemplified by the Type XXI, of which several were in operation in April 1945. This was still diesel-driven with *Schnorchels*, but had very powerful batteries indeed and a high underwater speed which could be continued for a long time. U-boats so equipped were very formidable weapons, as the only part of the vessel which need show above the water was the *Schnorchel*, and their speed would allow them to overtake convoys while submerged.

In addition a similar but smaller boat, the Mark XXIII, was produced which operated with success off the east coast of England from January 1945 onwards.

If the original programme had kept up to time, no less than 290 of the larger boats and 140 of the smaller should have been operating by February 1945. But the Allied strategic bombing and the laying of mines in the Baltic so delayed the projects that the new types were not able to play any significant part in the war.

The second type, which never actually came into service, was a true submarine: in other words, one which need never come to the surface. Its engines were driven by hydrogen peroxide, it had a high speed and again would have been very dangerous to the Allies.

If Hitler had put his full support behind the projects, if the best scientists and engineers had been employed to develop them, and if they had been given high priority in the fight for materials, both these new types might have been put into service much earlier, and the Allies would have been in sore straits. The results of a renewed Battle of the Atlantic fought with these new weapons would be difficult to forecast, and I cannot see, for example, the invasion of 1944 having been launched on time, if at all.

It was most fortunate that Hitler never understood the problems of the sea or the potentiality of a really serious attack by submarines on an island power which depended on imports for its life-blood.

When we consider electronic warfare the story is quite different, and the balance of advantage swings firmly on to the British side, due, as I have said, to the more intelligent use of the scientific effort available.

Taking the asdic first: the Germans had no active transmitter, so they were unable to get ranges of a target. They were slow, too, in producing counter-measures to the asdic, such as the air-bubble which aimed to deceive the operator. It is true that the U-boats were fitted with most efficient hydrophones which allowed them to get bearings of the propellor noises of ships and convoys at very long distances, but on balance again I think that the British were on top.

The story of the use of radar in the U-boat war is a strange one. The Germans had pioneered the development of radar for use against surface ships, whereas on the British side, the first employment of radar was almost entirely against aircraft, and its use against surface ships came almost as a casual bonus.

Yet when the fitting of British radar of short wavelength, both in all escorts and in some aircraft in late 1942, revolutionized the submarine war, the Germans, took a long time to produce a search receiver.

Later on, after a new search receiver proved disappointing, the German scientists came to the remarkable and untrue conclusion that the British must be picking up radiations from the old search receiver with which their boats were fitted for use against metre wavelength radar. As a result the inoffensive and useful 'Metox' was removed from all U-boats, which thus became even more unprepared for dealing with aircraft attacks.

The Leigh Light must also be mentioned in this context as this ingenious invention lit up U-boats on the surface at night and so gave aircraft a killing power all around the clock which they had not previously possessed. We have not yet heard of this device because the Wellington aircraft in which it was fitted did not have the endurance to escort North Atlantic convoys, and operated only on the Bay of Biscay patrols; but it was in full use in the spring of 1943. If it had been fitted to some of the V.L.R. Liberators, the U-boat successes against convoys would have been much reduced, since convoy air escort could have been achieved by night as well as by day.

As to the use of H/F D/F, it took the Germans a very long time to appreciate that ships were fitted with these invaluable devices, although they knew that there was a network of shore H/F D/F stations scattered around the Atlantic. We have seen that the escort groups usually got warning of impending attack, not only from the Admiralty, but also from their own H/F D/F sets which also helped them to decide from where the attack was most likely to come.

Of course, the whole system of wolf-pack attacks depended on radio transmissions on H/F. The Germans did not appreciate the advantages of brevity – it was easier to get a bearing of a long signal than of a short – and their messages were often unnecessarily long and contained detail which could easily have been omitted. Neither do I believe that it was essential for U-boats to report by radio just before they went in to attack; not only did this alert the escort but the reason for making the signal – avoidance of possible collisions – seemed ill-founded.

From all this will be seen my conviction that in electronic warfare the British had a great advantage which had much influence on the outcome of the struggle.

For a variety of reasons, the training of the escort groups during the winter of 1942–3 had suffered severely. It was a vicious circle. The terrible weather slowed the speed of the convoys, which took longer to reach their destinations. Thus the escorts had less time to make good the weather defects in harbour and to carry out the vital training needed: training which included not only the operation of the guns and depth-charges and of the detecting equipment but also training in the maintenance of the highly sophisticated electronic sets now being fitted.

It was no good having the finest depth-charge crews and most efficient plotting team if either the asdic or the radar was not working; and bad weather affected both. Bad weather damaged some escorts so severely that they could not sail with their group on the next convoy, as their repairs took long to complete. This involved changing escorts around from group to group, some-times at short notice, and group training inevitably suffered. We have already seen how important it was for the escort commander to know his ships well and for each to know instinctively what to do in every situation.

Training suffered too, because some individuals in the more senior ranks were not up to their job. Like Coastal Command, the Western Approaches had for some time been the Cinderella of the Navy; but Admiral Horton soon changed all that and was ruthless in weeding out the weak and replacing them by high-calibre officers. By the spring of 1943, when Horton had been in charge for some four months, the effect was already being felt. Groups were being kept more together and were learning to work as teams. Ships were able to use the excellent facilities at the shore bases for training in weapons and tactics.

The latter training especially was well catered for by a tactical school run by Captain G. H. Roberts in Liverpool, where captains of ships and aircraft and other officers were able to attend week-long courses and study convoy defence problems, and by small tactical schools at some bases where the results of actual convoys could be studied and the lessons learnt.

Groups began to be able to carry out exercises at sea before sailing to meet their convoy, and this made a tremendous differ-ence to the standard of training and the state of morale. Ships began to realize that they had effective weapons and equipment which, if properly used, could defeat the U-boats.

In a few vital weeks, standards rose from low to satisfactory and in some cases high levels; and this of course had a vital influence on the outcome of the battle.

It is interesting to compare this situation with that on the German side. A new U-boat, or one which had received a long refit or repair in Germany, would be subject to a most thorough training programme in the Baltic, ranging from individual firing of weapons to pack attacks on mock convoys. (Later in the war, these were badly disrupted by Bomber Command's mining of the Baltic.)

The initial stages of the Baltic training corresponded in some ways to the short courses for all Allied escorts, run at Tobermory under the guidance of Commodore Gilbert Stephenson. Here officers and men, some of whom had never seen the sea before, were quickly imbued with the elements of their new profession, using methods which were sometimes highly unconventional.

When, however, the U-boats were operating from bases in the Bay of Biscay, like La Pallice, St Nazaire and Lorient, the story seems to be quite different. I have read many books written by Germans on the U-boat war, and have never yet found any reference to training before sailing or to exercises after going to sea.

There are glowing descriptions of the return to harbour, the greeting by Dönitz or some other senior officer, the presentation of medals, and the bands and ceremonial. Then the U-boat seems to have been turned over to the maintenance staff at the base, whose job was to make it fit for the next operation as quickly and as thoroughly as possible. The crew were either sent on leave to Germany or were transferred *en bloc* to rest camps where they were able to enjoy the French environment. And there was no doubt that they needed a rest after a typical operation.

The reasons for the lack of training are probably many. I believe that over-confidence was one. The difficulty of providing training facilities at several French bases is another. Time between patrols was short and as much rest as possible was wanted. The minefields laid by British aircraft which required daily minesweeping must have been another reason, and finally came the danger from British aircraft engaged on sorties into the Bay.

Nevertheless I have a conviction, though no proof, that the lack of practice led to many failures in operations. Even in an account of one convoy, HX231, one reads of guns jamming, of failures to fire torpedoes, of torpedoes running in circles instead of straight, and of other defects.

I personally believe that the difference in standards of training between British escorts and German submarines was important; but not all submarine officers will agree with me.

As to the improvement in standards of Coastal Command training, the story is equally dramatic and is closely connected with the arrival of Sir John Slessor at Coastal headquarters in February 1943. In the first four months of that year the ratio of kills to U-boats was only 9 per cent: in other words out of every 100 U-boats sighted by aircraft of the Command, only nine were sunk. In May 1943, the figure rose to nearly 30 per cent, a tremendous difference and the result of a determined effort that all aircraft should exercise against submarine targets and practise every facet of the drill in the aircraft during the attack. Homing procedures improved, so that occasions when the aircraft failed to meet the convoy were very few, and communications with the escorts also got better. The state of affairs was transformed in a very short time.

Intelligence generally was of course extremely important, and the success or failure of the cryptographers played a very major part in the full intelligence picture, so I propose to discuss that aspect first.

It is difficult to form a judgement on the relative advantages gained by each side, because the German successes have been widely publicized, whereas British achievements can only be guessed from occasional indiscretions in documents in the Public Records Office, and from the cryptic allusions of Roskill in his naval history. Official policy is still, wrongly I believe, to keep this side of the war effort a deadly secret and it is therefore impossible to get any authentic information.

As we have seen, the Germans had some brilliant cryptographers, and from the start the British ciphers and codes were vulnerable to the expert. It was not until the end of May 1943 that the British ciphers became safe against decryption.

On the British side it is known that the submarine *U110* was captured intact by the destroyer *Bulldog* in May 1941, and that much invaluable intelligence material of every sort was found on board. What was just as important, the German crew had no idea that the boat had been captured – they thought that it had sunk as soon as they had abandoned ship – so that U-boat headquarters was unaware that so much important intelligence material had fallen into the hands of the enemy.

The whole operation had been brilliantly carried out; and the secrecy achieved was astonishing, for many officers and men in the *Bulldog* knew what had happened, as well as some survivors from sunken merchant ships. But even the official historian was unaware of the event until after he had completed his history!

As to the material captured, it is no secret that the Germans used a machine-type cipher, and it is a reasonable guess that the machine was among the material captured from the *U110*. I would assume, therefore, that from the time when our experts got the measure of the machine – and this would not take long – we were able to read the German signals, possibly until 8 March 1943, when as we have seen, the cryptographers went temporarily 'blind'. Presumably the Germans had then changed some features of the cipher machine.

The battle between the rival cryptographers evidently worked in waves. Sometimes one side was on top and sometimes the other. My belief, however, is that in general, and especially during the vital spring of 1943, the Germans had the superiority, which brought them very considerable advantages.

The intelligence picture was built up out of a range of different factors which contributed in varying degrees to the whole. Cryptography, clearly, was one. Interrogation of prisoners of war also yielded some very important information and the British had some skilled practitioners in the art. Espionage was obviously important, as were more mundane sources like the study of German newspapers and broadcasts, the reading of neutral papers and the information gleaned from agents and friends in neutral countries like Sweden and Portugal. The various resistance movements, especially the French organization, also contributed much information on U-boats.

Air reconnaissance of bases and building yards was vital if we were to know how many U-boats were being built and of what types. The high-flying Spitfire, specially converted to take photographs, did some magnificent work.

I am no intelligence expert, and it is therefore with some trepidation that I advance my opinion which is that in general intelligence, as opposed to cryptography, the British were far superior to the Germans.

Certainly U-boat prisoners were astonished by their interrogators' knowledge about the U-boat service, its personnel and its material. And in the tactical games in which we exercised the defence of convoys at the tactical school in Liverpool, we had excellent information as to enemy methods and we got to know the names and characteristics of the outstanding U-boat aces like old friends.

On the other hand, the German knowledge of British weapons and methods was surprisingly scanty and their general intelligence picture was far from complete.

The coming of the support groups was a potent factor in the battle. Taken alone, they were important assets, and when they also included an escort carrier with its anti-submarine planes and its fighters, they were very formidable indeed. Moreover when the weather in Iceland or Northern Ireland was such as to prevent flying from the bases there, the escort carriers could probably operate and thus help to keep the 'air gap' closed.

By the end of May, there were five support groups operating in the Atlantic, three of which had escort carriers attached, and the results were striking. When the support group was present, few merchant ships were sunk, and these were almost all from one convoy which came under very heavy attack indeed; and several U-boats were sunk.*

Of course, there were disadvantages to the support group system, which depended on milking the Home Fleet of the destroyers which were usually employed on convoys to North Russia, and on reducing the size of the regular escort groups to one which was too small to take on a wolf-pack with confidence.

Moreover the correct operation of support groups depended largely on good intelligence: of knowing which convoys were going to be attacked and on supporting them before the attack developed. It was unlucky that the cryptographers lost their ability to read the enemy messages just before the First Support Group joined the command in March; and their operation had to be arranged by intelligent anticipation and by the rather rough and ready methods of fixing submarines' positions from the chain of shore-based H/F D/F stations.

There can be no dispute that the support group system ran risks, and the tale of convoy HX231 battling its way with only six escorts through a large wolf-pack showed how great the risk was. But in surveying the whole period of April and May 1943, one can only conclude that in general the support groups managed to be in the right place at the right time, so ensuring that almost every convoy was given a reinforced and sometimes powerful defence. They contributed substantially to the victory.

I have left to the end of this chapter the effect of the provision of air escort to convoys and particularly to escort in the 'air gap' in mid-Atlantic which was filled, at least in daylight, by the arrival of the V.L.R. Liberators, operating from Iceland, Northern Ireland and, at the end of May, from Newfoundland.†

The reason for leaving this matter to the end is because, after

* Roskill in his Volume II, pages 380-1, gives a most interesting abstract of all the convoy passages of the period, with the details of the support groups present and the results.

† I have not considered the important air operations over the U-boat transit routes through the Bay of Biscay, because they did not substantially affect the issue until the summer of 1943.

much thought, it seems to me that out of the many factors which contributed to the victory, the provision of air escort for convoys which were threatened or under attack was probably the most important of all. Again the phrase 'threatened or under attack' will be noted, for there were simply not enough aircraft to give air escort to every convoy, and so again intelligence of the enemy intentions had a decisive effect on the effectiveness of the whole. I am sure that had the British cryptographers been reading German signals, air escort would have been provided for convoy HX231 on 4 April, and so greatly have hindered the assembly of Group *Löwenherz*.

With even one aircraft present, the U-boats were almost helpless and it was noticeable how they gradually dropped astern of a fast convoy due to their inability to use their high surface speed.

Then at dusk, when the aircraft left, the U-boats' job was not easy, especially if the convoy carried out an evasive turn after dark and so made attack more difficult.

Looking back, it will always remain a mystery to me that there was so much opposition to the provision of the comparatively few V.L.R. aircraft needed for Coastal Command, and that the opposition to the move was successful for so long.

It had been clearly demonstrated by 120 Squadron in December 1942, at what a great distance air escort could be provided for Atlantic convoys and with what effect. What is more, these magnificent Liberators were not particularly successful as night bombers. Yet it was not until April 1943 that 86 Squadron started to operate, and not until the end of May that ten aircraft were found to transfer to the Royal Canadian Air Force in Newfoundland; this finally and fully closed the 'air gap'.

Much credit must be given to Sir John Slessor (now Marshal of the Royal Air Force) who so quickly appreciated that close air escort of threatened and attacked convoys must take precedence over all other demands on his available forces. He was also quick to understand that an aircraft surface-ship team was the most effective submarine-killer combination.

As for the aircrew of 120 and 86 Squadrons, history should not forget that these comparatively few individuals should be accorded as much credit as any others concerned in the victory over Dönitz and his U-boats.

I hope that I will be forgiven for one final quotation from the official historian's remarks on the crisis of the battle:

> 'In all the long history of sea warfare there has been no parallel to this battle, whose field was thousands of square miles of ocean, and to which no limits in time or space could be set. In its intensity, and in the certainty that its outcome would decide the issue of the war, the battle may be compared with the Battle of Britain in 1940. Just as Goering then tried with all the forces of the Luftwaffe to gain command of the skies over Britain, so now did Dönitz seek to gain command over the Atlantic with his U-boats. And the men who defeated him – the crews of the little ships, of the air escorts and of our tiny force of long-range aircraft – may be justly immortalized alongside "the few" who won the 1940 battle of the air.'

# Bibliography

## Main Sources

Brennecke, J., trs. by R. H. Stevens, *The Hunters and the Hunted*. London: Starke 1958

Busch, Harald, trs. by L. R. P. Wilson, *U-Boats at War*. London: Putnam 1955

Creighton, Rear-Admiral Sir Kenelm, *Convoy Commodore*. London: Kimber 1956

Dönitz, Grand Admiral Karl, trs. by R. H. Stevens with David Woodward, *Memoirs*. London: Weidenfeld & Nicolson 1959

Kerr, G. G., *Business in Great Waters*. London: Faber & Faber 1951

Price, Alfred, *Aircraft versus Submarine*. London: Kimber 1973

Roskill, S. W., *The Secret Capture*. London: Collins 1959

Roskill, S. W., *The War at Sea*, 1939–45 Vol. II. London: H.M. Stationery Office 1957

Rutter, Owen, *Red Ensign*. London: Hale 1942

Saunders, H. G., *Valiant Voyaging*. London: Faber & Faber 1949

Schaeffer Heinz, trs. by George Edinger and Godfrey Wilson, *U-Boat 977*. London: Kimber 1952

Scholfield, B. B. and Martyn, L. F., *Rescue Ships*. London: Blackwood 1968

Seth, Ronald, *The Fiercest Battle*. London: Hutchinson 1961

# Index